How to Write Well

How to Write Well

A guide for health and social care students

June Keeling, Hazel M. Chapman, and Julie Williams

Mc Graw Hill Education   Open University Press

Open University Press
McGraw-Hill Education
McGraw-Hill House
Shoppenhangers Road
Maidenhead
Berkshire
England
SL6 2QL

email: enquiries@openup.co.uk
world wide web: www.openup.co.uk

and Two Penn Plaza, New York, NY 10121-2289, USA

First published 2013

A catalogue record of this book is available from the British Library

ISBN-13: 978-0-335-24493-5
ISBN-10: 0-335-24493-9
eISBN: 978-0-335-24494-2

Library of Congress Cataloging-in-Publication Data
CIP data applied for

Typeset by Aptara, Inc.

Praise for this book

"This book is aimed at students, but I am sure that it has an audience beyond that - we all need help and encouragement to write. Full of practical advice and examples, this book will help you to find a writing strategy that works for you and to develop your own style. Some simple but very effective ideas are used such as: making writing a normal activity; just keeping going; and not necessarily starting at the beginning."

Roger Watson, Professor of Nursing,
University of Hull, UK

"The focus of this book is on how to write well. As I have argued previously, we all need to be reminded of the skills required in order to make a difference to our patient, clients and their carers' lives. Lifelong learning is the way that we update our knowledge, skills and competencies. But in order to do this effectively we need to have the right skill set. The ability to write well is fundamental to our personal and professional learning, and this is regardless of what stage we are in our careers. Writing is a skill that we use every day, be it an email to a friend or an assignment for a course. With practice we can develop and refine this essential skill. I particularly like the way the authors encourage us to be critical of our writing; this is also something that we can offer to others as critical friends."

Sian E Maslin-Prothero, Professor of Nursing (Clinical),
School of Nursing & Midwifery and
Sir Charles Gairdner Hospital,
Edith Cowan University, Western Australia

Contents

Contributors

Hazel M. Chapman, RGN, RNMH/DipHE, BSc(Psychology), MA(Education) is a senior lecturer at the University of Chester. Her main teaching and research interests are human interactions within health care. She is currently presenting her findings on research into student nurse attitudes of respect towards service users and completing research into the experience of health care consultations for people with a learning disability. Hazel has almost 15 years of experience in nursing education and enjoys working with students at all levels. Hazel is co-ordinating editor of *New Scholar*, the journal for undergraduates in health and social care at the University of Chester.

Elizabeth Cooper is a registered nurse, working within as a senior lecturer, with a specific interest in the practice learning. She has worked with learners for 12 years, with an increasing passion for supporting learners within an environment of professional education. Currently, she is the faculty co-ordinator for practice and skills learning.

Dr June Keeling is a senior lecturer at the University of Chester. She is a qualified nurse and midwife who has had the privilege of working in both New Zealand and the UK, enjoying a wide range of approaches to education and practice. She co-ordinates modules at undergraduate and postgraduate level, being involved in the process of developing degree courses, curricula design and implementation. June's main research interest is in the use of violence within relationships.

Dr Carol Lewis-Roylance has worked in higher education for the past 15 years as a lecturer, researcher and study skills tutor. She is currently employed as a DSA Assessor/Specialist Tutor at Glyndwr University in North Wales. Her specialist area of interest is the social history of medicine during the inter-war period.

Jane Quigley, senior lecturer in the Faculty of Health at the University of Chester, teaches on foundation degree, undergraduate and postgraduate level courses specifically in areas such as mentorship and leadership in the NHS. Her main area of interest is in practice and student placements and support of student learning.

Victoria Ridgway is a senior lecturer at the University of Chester. She qualified as an adult nurse in 1993 and worked in acute care, but has worked in higher education since 2002. Her interests are vast but predominantly centre around teaching and supporting undergraduate/postgraduate health and social care students in research. Her own research interests focus on care of the older person.

Pat Talbot is a senior lecturer at the University of Chester. She started her career in adult nursing, moving into learning disability nursing and then into teaching. She has a Masters degree in community care from Keele University. Her interests include physical health needs of people with learning disabilites and she also enjoys the process of helping students to develop their academic skills.

Dr Julie Williams is Director of Nurse Education at the University of Lincoln. Her academic career began as a nurse lecturer at the University of Liverpool before moving to the University of Chester as Head of Department in the Faculty of Health and Social Care. With a PhD in Educational Research from the University of Lancaster she is interested in studying discipline-specific academic identity formation and curriculum quality and development.

Acknowledgements

We would like to express our gratitude to all those who have contributed to this book. We would also like to thank those at Open University Press, especially Rachel Crookes, for their patience and guidance in the development of this project.

June would like to thank John, Max, Joel and Natasha for their endless patience, humour and space to work. June would like to also thank her parents, Ronnie and Jean, for their enthusiasm and passion for education – a gift for life. Thanks also to friends and colleagues for all their contributions.

Hazel would like to thank all her family, especially Myra, Matthew, Rachel, Wayne, Joe and Hannah; thanks also to Mike White, Andy Lovell, Ros Bramwell, Elizabeth Mason-Whitehead, Annette McIntosh-Scott, Lynda Rosie and June Keeling for their mentorship and support.

Julie would like to thank colleagues both past and present with a special thank you to her family and friends for all their constant support and unfailing sense of humour.

List of tables

List of figures

1

Introduction

June Keeling, Julie Williams and Hazel Chapman

The aim of this book is to demystify academic writing for undergraduate students in health and social care education. You are probably required to submit several assignments throughout your programme of study, which may take different formats such as a written essay, a poster or a dissertation. The allocation of marks for your assignments will be primarily dependent upon two factors: content and academic writing. This book focuses on the many aspects that impact on the quality of academic writing and will help you to develop the essential skills required for your undergraduate level study and to achieve success. Academic writing is a skill that develops with practice and therefore the book takes you through a step-by-step guide of how to improve your academic writing, thereby enabling you to improve your own writing skills.

The book will guide you through different styles of writing, each style addressed in a separate chapter providing clarity and differentiation between the styles. The chapters will not only provide details about a different writing style, but also show examples of work and a list of tips for you to work through. A critical analysis of work is offered in each chapter, giving you an instant idea of what is required, helping you to engage with 'real life' writing.

This book is unique in that the authors provide actual examples of academic writing to guide you in your own writings. As such, this book endeavours to enhance your academic writing skills and increase your depth of understanding of academic writing within health and social care education. The book also provides a template for you to critique your own work.

You will be expected to develop your writing skills in order to progress to the next academic level. Therefore, it is crucial that you engage with academic writing at the earliest opportunity. These issues, and more, are explored within the book. The focus of the book is aimed at all students studying health and social care related programmes of study. In addition, it specifically addresses the development of students' writing skills for both academic and professional purposes.

The book is intended for a wide audience ranging from those who have limited writing skills through to and including more experienced novice writers. Importantly, it also includes those who have specific learning needs and addresses the needs of people who use English as a second language. The book explores different styles of writing to enable the student to recognise their own strengths and then work with this to maximise their output.

How to use the book

The book is divided into nine clear and distinct chapters. Each chapter addresses a different topic in a clear and user friendly format. As academic writing skills are a fundamental component of any education programme within the health and social care arena, each chapter will inform you of a different aspect of academic writing. Therefore, we would recommend that you work through all the book chapters one by one. However, as there is no sequential approach to the chapters, you can start at whichever chapter you choose. The book will encourage you to engage with the chapters by listing a number of points throughout each chapter to highlight key concepts. Additionally, each chapter uses a series of exercises, encouraging you to 'go the extra mile' by becoming critical of your own work. Complete each exercise and study the key points from each chapter.

Structure of the book

In *Chapter 2*, you will read about the psychology of writing and through understanding yourself learn to produce your best writing, on time and as part of your everyday life. You can explore why you want to write and use this as motivation to write. Even when you want to write, you may still have trouble getting started, but this chapter will help you to break down the psychological barriers, so that your new behaviours make you feel more confident about your writing. You may find the section on creating your own writing space a useful place to begin. This chapter will help you formulate a plan to reduce your writing into manageable chunks. You will use these learned skills in all your writing activities. Using feedback on your writing is important for future success, so there are activities to help you with this.

Chapter 3 provides you with information related to the skills required and the rules to follow when writing whilst studying at university. It provides guidance on how best to differentiate between standard English and colloquial English and the basic rules of sentence structure, common approaches and styles. Furthermore, it gives you some useful hints and tips to make writing easier and identifies the do and don'ts.

Chapter 4 addresses the specific writing skills required by identifying the difference between studying in school or college and what is expected at university. It offers clear examples of the different techniques that can be used for academic and/or professional writing. The chapter clarifies the differences between the levels of academic writing and guides you to various activities to practise these. As you progress with your studies within health and social care, you will need to achieve at different academic levels, including levels 4, 5 and 6.

Chapter 5 explores reflection as it relates to your personal and professional life. It presents various models of reflection and within each model you will find examples on how to apply these in practice. Reflection can make you more aware of your practice and help you to feel more confident in yourself in general.

Chapter 6 examines the skills needed to enable you to write safe and effective service user records within the health and social care environment. It provides useful advice on how to prepare reports that are structured, well written and precise. These reports will accurately present the information in a relevant format as pertinent to the reader. The chapter also addresses the legal and ethical aspects of writing reports in health and social care practice.

Chapter 7 explores and identifies the variety of formats used for assessment purposes. Regardless of the programme of study within health and social care, an increasing emphasis is placed upon writing or oral presentations as key components for assessment. Therefore, oral presentations and other types of assessment such as posters, dissertations, oral exams and portfolios are explored in this chapter. For each of these formats we provide examples and key tips for consideration.

In *Chapter 8* five students reflect on their personal experiences and tell their stories about how they engaged with writing at university. This chapter is a practical demonstration of how students follow very different paths to engage, understand and become masters of their own writing.

Finally, in *Chapter 9,* we have drawn together key elements from each chapter to help you reflect on what you have learned. Through a range of activities you will consolidate the learning you have gathered from the chapters within this book.

2

Preparing to write

Hazel M. Chapman

This chapter explores the following topics:

- The psychology of writing
- How to reduce stress and anxiety
- Why writing is important for learning
- Why do you want to write well?
- A space of one's own
- Getting started and finishing well
- Reading for writing – and other learning resources
- Using feedback and accessing support

Introduction

This chapter begins by looking at how your thoughts and feelings about writing, especially writing for assessment, can affect your behaviour. Through understanding what makes you write or prevents you from writing, you can gain control over your writing behaviours, the behaviours that are key to your ultimate performance. This chapter shows the small, simple steps you can take in order to achieve your writing potential. By exploring how to break down the barriers to writing, such as stress and anxiety, this chapter shows how writing can eventually become just another activity, and even an enjoyable habit. We discuss the reasons why writing is important for helping you to learn, and help you to explore your own reasons for wanting to write. This will help you to keep writing, even when you are finding it challenging. The environment you work in is important for developing good writing habits and enabling you to write well, so the chapter discusses how you can create your own writing den and find your favourite writing haunts. Practical tips, such as where to find your ideas from, how to start writing, how to finish your writing session, and how to plan writing for assessment are included. Suggestions on using different sources of information and inspiration for your writing, how to use feedback to improve your writing, and how to get the most from university student support services are given. Writing is an important part of your life when you are studying in health and social care. This chapter helps you to put it into perspective alongside the rest of your life, so that you can approach the act of writing without fear, and develop your writing skills to achieve your full potential in your chosen field within health and social care.

The psychology of writing

Psychology is the study of the mind, and of how we interact with other people and the world around us (Hayes 2010). It focuses on how we think, feel and behave. Although they are not separate in real life, understanding the ways in which behaviours, emotions or thoughts affect each other will help you to identify more and less helpful patterns in your psychology of writing. By understanding your patterns of thinking, feeling and behaving when preparing to write, you will gain control over your writing.

You may realise that your thinking abilities are being developed and assessed through the process of writing, but it is also your motivation and temperament that are being tested, which is important for your professional life in health and social care. Generally, the stronger your belief in our own ability to organise and carry out necessary steps in order to achieve a certain goal (self-efficacy), the more likely you are to keep trying to achieve or improve something, and the more quickly you will overcome disappointment if you experience setbacks (Bandura 1997). Self-efficacy is an important part of the way you see yourself, especially in relation to your writing. Prior experience of success in writing will give you a stronger sense of self-efficacy, as will seeing other people working hard to achieve their writing goals. Having supportive people around you who encourage your effort and achievements is also important, as is your emotional response to success and setbacks. Remember, everybody who is accepted on to a university programme in health and social care has achieved the academic levels required for that course of study. So even if you find writing challenging, you have the ability to achieve at that level, as long as you put in the necessary work. Therefore, any written assessment is testing your motivation to keep trying and working, even when you find the task difficult. This motivation and self-efficacy is an important consideration in terms of both academic and professional progress.

Writing is not just a way of testing what we have learned, but an essential part of the learning process. This process changes our understanding and helps us to develop new skills and perspectives (Nunez and Freeman 1999). When we achieve this successfully and gain positive feedback, it strengthens our belief in our ability to write and learn. When the feedback advises us to work on aspects of our writing, it is those students who see this as a positive aid to their learning and use it to improve who gain the most from their writing. So, before preparing to write, it is important to think about our prior experience of writing and how it makes us feel.

Lynda's first essay

Lynda did not do very well at school, despite picking ideas up easily, and left at the age of 16 to become an apprentice hairdresser. After having her first child, Lynda realised that she wanted to be a physiotherapist, but needed better qualifications, so she took part-time courses to gain the entry requirements to study physiotherapy at university. With a small child, she knew it was going to be challenging, but felt that her strong motivation to become a physiotherapist and her life experience would help her to get through. She spoke to all her family about needing support for the next three years so that she could achieve her goal of becoming a qualified physiotherapist. Lynda started university a few weeks ago and has made some friends already, but she is worried that when she submits her first essay it will not be good enough. She has chatted with her friends in the group and they all seem to feel the same way.

Activity 2.1 Your psychological responses to writing

When you have to submit a piece of written work for a deadline, does your behaviour fit into any of the following patterns?

(a) You would try to forget all about the essay because whenever you think about it you feel anxious.

(b) You would talk about it often with your friends, as it makes you feel better to know that you're all in the same boat, but you don't need to do anything else because no one else is.

(c) When the lecturer talks about the essay in class, you feel fine and understand it, but you can't remember what was said afterwards, when you think about starting to write, so you put it off until you can talk to someone about what you were told.

(d) You decide that your belief that you could do this course was over-optimistic and that you cannot achieve the required level without causing problems for yourself and your family.

(e) You leave it until the last minute, then, under pressure, cobble something together that you hope will be good enough for a pass, but certainly does not reflect your ability or potential as a student.

(f) You avoid the essay and your lecturers altogether and don't submit anything.

(g) You make a plan of all the things that you need to do, then start to do them one after the other, making sure that you always have some work to do in your free periods, lunchtimes, before a late shift, after an early shift, or between other commitments. That way, when you take time out for personal and family activities you don't feel anxious or guilty and can enjoy them.

Suggested strategies to get you started

Here are some suggested strategies for dealing with each of the different responses outlined in Activity 2.1. See which one fits with your behaviour the closest and which strategy would work best for you.

Table 2.1 Suggested strategies to get you started

Your response	Suggested strategy
(a)	Open your document or notepad and spend ten minutes writing down all your ideas so that you have made a start – make sure you build on it.
(b)	Focus on why you want to write and why you are taking this course. Think about the health or social care professional you want to become. Think about the people you spend time with – are they really supporting you?
(c)	Make sure you look at the subject matter of lectures and the assessment brief beforehand. In the lectures, write notes that you understand and look over them afterwards to make sure you still understand them. If you have any queries after looking through the module resources, contact your lecturer about them.
(d)	Just keep going, possibly after a short break to think about why this is important to you. Reward yourself for small achievements – a cup of tea at the end of a paragraph, for example.
(e)	Focus on the benefits of learning through writing. The mark you achieve is not a judgement of you as a person; it is an assessment of how well your learning is progressing. Effort and organisation are important. Set yourself small writing tasks and fit writing time into (almost) every day for them.
(f)	Find the assessment brief and any notes about it. Write your name and the title on a piece of paper or document. If you have subheadings, put them in. Write down any ideas that you have – if you need information, make a note of what is missing, but carry on. As soon as you have a plan or draft, if possible send it to your lecturer for feedback. If you still can't resolve this, write down what you are having difficulties with and make an appointment to discuss it with your lecturer.
(g)	Well done – you have a good writing habit. Make sure you build some rewards into your writing activity and have a good work–life balance.

Barriers to learning

We learn coping mechanisms, or patterns of thoughts, feelings and behaviour, early on in our lives to help us to deal with difficult situations. We tend to fall into these patterns of coping whenever we face similar difficult situations in our lives. Under stress, it could be easy to fall into an avoidant way of coping with the stress of writing an assignment. If you don't work out a strategy to make the most of your abilities and to write your assignments in good time, you will put yourself under pressure. If you find more important or more urgent activities that help you to avoid writing and any related fears of academic failure, although you can escape the stress in the short term, it will build up and reach crisis point. University is adult education and you are aiming to become a health or social care professional, where maturity and self-motivation are essential, but there are similarities of environment and expectations between university and school. These similarities could make it easy for you to revert back to the patterns of thinking, feeling and behaving that you have 'grown out of'.

When you feel stressed, you produce an adrenalin response that is normally short lived. However, if you are not able to face the threat and deal with it straightaway, you keep producing stress hormones which cause anxiety. Anxiety is uncomfortable and unpleasant, so most people avoid things that make them anxious. Any past experience of failure will reinforce your anxiety and can increase the avoidant behaviour. Practice placements can give you a sense of security, particularly at the beginning of your programme, when your knowledge base is not under so much pressure, making it easy to use them to avoid thinking about your writing. The more you avoid doing any work towards your essay, the greater the anxiety when you do think about it. Finally, you will either cram six months' worth of study into about 24 hours, or you will be unable to submit on time, with consequent effects on your academic progress.

Stress is a barrier to considered thought or academic analysis. Stress demands action, but thought requires concentration. Under stress you are likely to behave in an instinctive, not strategic, way. In the short term you may find other activities make you feel you have achieved something, or take your mind off the assignment you need to write. This is because immediate rewards are more effective in reinforcing behaviours than delayed rewards, and because you see writing as a bad experience in some way. Often, in health and social care practice, rewards are immediate: a service user's smile or 'thank you' or a 'well done' from a colleague. When you try to think about and write notes for your assignment, the output can seem very small for the effort and time expended, and the fears about eventual achievement may be greater than the relief of producing some work. So you need some strategies to help you, and you need to develop your own motivation for writing. In the following sections, a few simple strategies for reducing barriers to writing are suggested.

How to reduce stress and anxiety

Put writing in its place

- Treat it like any other task and fit it into your day.
- Writing does not define you, it is a skill that you can develop.
- Writing is a tool to structure your ideas, identify what you need to know and demonstrate your knowledge for assessment.
- Carry a small piece of work with you so that you can write wherever you are.

If you regularly get to the end of you day and you have not managed to fit in even 30 minutes of writing, then you need to look at how you spend your time and reorganise your priorities. If you feel as if you are working hard but you have little to show for it, try the following strategies:

- Plan what you are going to do in small manageable tasks.
- Plan when you are going to do it within your daily life.
- Set your next session's writing goals a few minutes before you finish your current writing session.
- Tick off each task as you complete it.

You will be writing in some capacity for the rest of your life. Health and social care professionals need to keep detailed records, write reports, referrals and letters, even conference presentations and academic papers. They often have to fit documentation into a busy practice day, and writing to gain further qualifications around their working life. You cannot put your normal life on hold in order to write – you need to adapt and make a plan.

Planning for writing

Not having enough time is the most common reason people give for not starting an assignment, but very few people would leave the house without brushing their teeth, or not find time to buy food or go to work. As a student of health and social care, writing is your work just as much as gaining skills for practice. Health and social care professionals are expected to use knowledge to support their decisions and interventions in practice.

Planning skills

- Set short-term and long-term goals. Aim to have all your assignments ready before the submission date, but make sure you have small tasks towards that goal planned for most days.
- Divide your time into the goals that have to be achieved. Set smaller goals for each day or week, but make sure you leave extra time in case of unforeseen events.
- Set yourself deadlines so that you know most of your work will be completed well in advance of the submission date.
- Plan to write in the hours around your shifts and practice placements. Health professional programmes are based on the expectation that you will study several hours a day in addition to both university attendance and practice placements.
- Make a few notes about the topic before lectures, so that you can follow the lecturer's ideas and feel confident to ask questions.
- After lectures, write down the key points you have learned and plan your follow-up studying.
- If you have more than half-an-hour for lunch, use the rest of the time available to find books or articles, write a paragraph, check the assessment brief online, format your references or make notes on a relevant topic.

Activity 2.2 Setting goals

In the box below is a generic sample plan to break down your writing into achievable goals. You may need to tackle each section separately if the work is large, or add more sections. Take the piece of writing you need to do and use it to plan your writing task

Title of essay/presentation:
Tasks for each section:
 	
• Identify key sources of information – write reference in required format.
• Write relevant notes.
• Organise ideas into key points.
• Write each section.
 	
Overall tasks:
 	
• Read and edit to ensure logical progression of ideas.
• Write links at the beginning and end of paragraphs/sections/chapters to aid flow of points.
• Proofread to ensure best presentation of ideas in writing (check for sentence structure, spelling, punctuation). Writing should be clear and concise.
 	
Sections to be written (paragraphs/sections/ slides/chapters):
 	
1 Introduction – key points
2 Section heading
  2.1 Part one
  2.2 Part two
  2.3 Part three
3 Section heading
  3.1 Part one
  3.2 Part two
  3.3 Part three
4 Section heading
  4.1 Part one
  4.2 Part two
  4.3 Part three
5 Conclusion – key points
	Date for completion by

The planning may not be as precise as you would like. After all, if you knew exactly what the whole exercise involved then writing it would be easy. However, by setting smaller goals you will reduce the task down to size, making it less daunting and easier to fit into your busy schedule.

Make writing rewarding

If thinking about writing produces negative emotions, you need to change your writing behaviours. Seeing your writing as a positive way to improve your learning and practice, writing little and often so that your task is manageable and rewarding yourself for small achievements will make you feel happier about your writing. This is because new associations will be made with the behaviour of writing and the consequences of that behaviour. To strengthen the positive connections in the short term, plan rewards for your writing. By rewarding yourself for writing a paragraph, editing a section, writing notes from a text or article, or writing a plan, over a period of time you will find that you have changed how you feel about writing. A reward is whatever you enjoy, so write a list of your favourite things and use them as your rewards. I have been known to cut up a miniature bar of chocolate into about 50 pieces and eat one piece after every 50 words written.

Activity 2.3 Reward yourself

List your favourite rewards in the table below – it can be your favourite food, drink, activity, television programme, or whatever you like.

My rewards

Keep rewarding your small writing achievements and they will grow into big ones. For the really big achievements, like submitting an essay or a chapter draft, you might encourage your friends and family to take you out for a meal or to the cinema. Eventually, writing will become a reward in itself as you begin to enjoy those periods of creativity. Once you start to enjoy writing, you will be rewarded by a feeling that you know more, by positive feedback and better marks from your lecturers, and by a feeling of being in control of your own future.

The next section looks at the reasons why writing is important, and then encourages you to explore your own reasons for wanting to write well. When you do find writing challenging, read over these sections to increase your motivation and self-efficacy. After that, you will be encouraged to prepare or select a writing environment to suit your needs because you need to break any negative associations and build pleasure into your writing habit.

Why writing is important for learning

Although the rewards of academic achievement are not immediate, they do open some really important doors and allow you to change your life. Writing is also a way of showing your knowledge and opinions to their best advantage, so that lecturers and ultimately other health and social care professionals will take notice of what you say. Writing for academic achievement is an apprenticeship that can lead to writing to influence the views and opinions of others, whether within your own field or in positions of power.

Being able to understand and remember information is very important for all health and social care students because of the 'theory – practice gap', one aspect of which is the difficulty in applying theoretical knowledge to clinical practice. Writing is not just something we do to pass an assessment; it is a way of helping us to develop and access the knowledge we need to be competent in practice. Writing forces your mind to process information so that you are able to retrieve it when it is relevant and use it appropriately. This enables you to build stronger neurological pathways (Bee and Boyd 2011) to more complex mental representations of your discipline which are quicker to access, allowing you to apply them when making critical decisions. Writing is not a separate activity to learning. To learn from any experience or information you need to: perceive it (take in information through our senses); attend to it (focus on that incoming information); remember it (encode it into your long-term memory); and be able to recall it in relevant situations (make connections with other relevant knowledge and experience) (Martin et al. 2010). When you are caring for someone and you remember relevant knowledge to apply in that situation, it shows that you are making connections with theory to develop your professional practice.

Have you ever sat in a lecture or seminar and realised you have not heard what was being said, or read the same page for 20 minutes without taking any of it in? You feel you have put in time and effort, but your mind is not attending to the information. Finding a way to structure the information – writing simple, colourful notes or diagrams, for example – helps you to focus on what is being said in lectures or books and to build connections with other ideas. All of us have countless mental representations (or schemas) of the world that are shaped by our experiences and the sense we have made of them. We tend to notice and understand new information using schemas that we have already developed (Martin et al. 2010). To gain understanding, we always have to go back to what we do understand and make connections with it.

The act of writing down your thoughts, whatever medium you use, forces you to 'make sense' of them, to build an understanding of them. This 'deep processing' of information means you encode it and connect it with other memories for storage in your long-term memory. These associations between the new information you assimilate and what you already know allows you to retrieve the new information in relation to a variety of different contexts. Some ideas you write about related to people with an intellectual disability, for example, may also be relevant when considering health or social care interventions for people with long-term illness. Writing also allows you to make new connections with other knowledge, and manipulate it for use in other settings such as practice. When you are preparing an assignment, writing notes about relevant theory and organising your ideas helps you to understand them, whether you use mind mapping (Buzan 2011; see Chapter 8: Activity 8.4) or other techniques to help you (Paschler et al. 2008).

Why do you want to write well?

In addition to these general motivations to write, you will have your own personal reasons for wanting to write well and thereby achieve your academic and professional goals. You will want to pass assignments and gain your qualifications; you will want to present your ideas in job interviews and professional meetings; you will want to communicate with other professionals to ensure that your service users receive the best care. However, what are your own personal motivations to succeed? Do you want to be a good role model for a younger sibling, child or other family member? Do you want to overcome a barrier that has stopped you achieving your potential in the past? Do you have a life goal that is very important to you? Do you want to make sure that people like your grandmother/ grandfather, parent, sibling, child, or friend receive better care? Do you want to feel proud of your academic achievements?

Activity 2.4 Reasons to write

In the box below, list all the reasons why you want to write and successfully complete your professional education programme.

Next time you have difficulty in getting yourself motivated have a look back at this list and refresh your enthusiasm for getting on with your writing. Add to the list when you find new reasons to write.

A space of one's own

When you write, it should be as pleasant an experience as possible. This section makes some suggestions to help you make your writing environment functional and inviting, or to find a place that suits you. We all need space to think – a little haven where we can, for a short while at least, shut out everything except what's going on inside our mind. Having a writing den provides us with a setting that we associate with writing. In developing that association, we are less likely to waste time settling down and getting started. So having your own space makes it easier for you to write because you get into the habit of writing there.

That's not all though. You can also change the behaviour of people you share your living space with. After all, some people around you may not realise how academically demanding health and social care professional programmes are. When you are in your writing den, you can make it clear that you are not to be disturbed except in emergencies. You are at work. Of course you have to stick to your own rules and be firm until people really get the message. This can take a bit of time, so be self-disciplined and don't give in to the temptations of your family and friends. If they really care, they will want you to achieve your own goals. Of course you have to have some family time and fun time, but by making it clear to yourself and others when you mean to write you will have no excuse not to do it, and you can enjoy your leisure time more.

The best thing about having your own writing space is that you can design it to suit yourself. You can have a separate room with a 'Do not disturb' sign on the door; or an alcove with its own lighting and shelves that allows you to keep an eye on children, for example. Whatever your space is like, you will need the following:

- at least one small shelf for textbooks (some key reference texts, plus the ones you have out of the library for your current writing project)
- a drawer to store your current project in
- a cupboard for folders and notepads
- sockets and a shelf for your laptop or PC
- good lighting
- somewhere to keep stationery, pens and other equipment
- a comfortable chair
- wi-fi is quite useful.

Activity 2.5 Design your own writing den

In the space below, have a go at drawing your own writing den. What room will you put it in? What furniture is already there? What furniture and equipment do you need? Use your imagination and plan for the writer you will become.

Now add any furniture and equipment you need (including textbooks) to your present wish list. Look out for stationery and small furniture in sales and make sure you ask for the things you want for birthdays and other special occasions.

If you have difficulty in working at home or just need the routine of leaving the house every day, then you need to seek out the best place for your writing. A laptop or tablet is ideal for working on as it takes up little room. If you find a free wi-fi spot you will also be able to access articles and e-books, as well as any university-provided online learning resources. However, nothing is easier than a notebook and pen. If you just want to make notes from a textbook, plan an assignment or reflect on practice (making sure you protect confidentiality), then they are perfectly suited to the task (and ideal for quick access in the practice placement). If you have textbooks and articles on an e-reader, you will need this as well, and it is much lighter than one or more thick textbooks. If you have a long train journey every day or once a week, this is an ideal opportunity to write and to plan your writing activity. The library is a good place to study as it is near to all the resources you need, has dedicated PCs and laptops and is generally handy for lectures and meetings. Although traditionally libraries are quiet places, some can be a little noisy, especially at busy times, and they may not suit you. In which case, you might like a particular café or even a burger bar (particularly if you find one with a free wi-fi connection). Select your haunt carefully and consider the following points:

- You should feel welcome but not obliged to join in general conversation.
- You should feel physically comfortable in terms of your table and chair, temperature and access to food, drink and toilet facilities.
- The lighting should suit you.
- There should not be too many distractions (pool tables, games machines, fun-loving friends, loud music).
- You should feel happy when you walk in.

Once you have chosen your writing haunt, make sure you are disciplined and set yourself goals to achieve while you are there. If you find that people start to seek you out there or you become too chatty with other patrons, you will need either to tell people that you go there to work or look for a new den. Remember, writing should be a pleasure and you should like the place you write in, but you still need to be self-disciplined about achieving your goals.

Getting started and finishing well

Let's not start at the beginning (and let's finish in the middle)

How often, when you are sitting down to write, do you know what you want to say but have difficulty with the opening line? You may know, for instance, that you want to describe an incident in your practice placement or work, but you are supposed to write about the background theory first – and that's the problem. Don't worry. Just start with the part that you want to write (or find easier to write). Once you have unlocked your inner writer, your urge to write will be much stronger. That will help you to overcome any feelings of being 'blocked', those feelings we have when we don't quite know what to say or how to say it. When you do get stuck, either because you don't have the information to hand or you don't understand it, don't let this distract you. Just make a note in the margin to remind you what you need to find out and move on to something that you *can* write about. Remember, you don't need to write to start writing – you can draw, you can mind map, you can list and you can audio-record your thoughts.

Alternative ways of thinking about writing

- Visual thinking – some people find it easier to think in terms of images rather than writing. Even though writing is the ultimate task, you can organise your ideas first and encourage processing of information by drawing pictures of the ideas you read about and think about.
- Mind mapping is a combination of visual thinking and organisation of ideas. It can be very useful in enabling you to write down ideas as you have them, and then connect them up in a way that helps you to plan your writing (see Chapter 8). It is also useful in helping you to organise your learning when revising for examinations.
- List the main topics – this stops you from writing everything you know about someone with a learning disability, say, rather than discussing the effects of the Michael Report (Michael and Richardson, 2008) on health care provision for someone with tuberous sclerosis.
- Keep an audio-recorder with you to record your writing ideas on the go – it can often be an easier way of getting started.
- You will eventually need to write, but if you find other ways of unlocking your ideas more appealing then start with them. You can move on to writing once you know what you want to write about.

Having a plan for your written work helps and checking it with your lecturer can prevent wasting time on topics which are not relevant to an assignment. Within the plan, though, there's no reason why you shouldn't start with section four before going back to section two, as long as you make sure they all flow together in a logical order as part of your editing process. In fact it is often helpful to write at least part of your introduction when you have completed the rest of your writing so that you can make sure it matches up with your conclusion.

Remember that your mind can become fatigued, so build up the amount of time you spend writing. You might just start with 30-minute writing sessions, as long as they are regular (once or twice a day). Five or ten minutes before your writing time is due to end, make sure you write notes about what else you want to write about and the next steps in your writing. This is often the most fruitful part of the writing process, so always remember to do it. You can also use the notes you have made in the writing process about things you need to look up to direct your next writing activity. By using this very simple tactic of always keeping a note of what you want to achieve next, you will never waste time. The feeling of being productive and in control of your writing will go a long way towards reducing any fears you may have about not getting your essay written. Above all, it means you will have something to show your lecturer in tutorials, so that the feedback you are given is more precise and relevant to you.

Reading for writing (and other sources of inspiration)

The internet can be a useful place to look for ideas and give you a start in looking for information. Using general search engines such as Google enables you to access lots of sources of information. However, this information could be irrelevant, incorrect or simply inappropriate for an academic course. It should be used carefully and only as a starting point. It is not appropriate to use information aimed at the general public to inform academic writing. Use your library search engines and relevant academic databases (such as CINAHL, PsycINFO, PubMed, SocINDEX) to access relevant articles and textbooks to support your writing. Searching for literature is a skill in itself. You will often find library staff very helpful, and your university will probably offer a guide to assist you, but like all skills it takes practice to develop.

Whatever level you are studying at, you need to read some basic textbooks. They should explain ideas or knowledge at a level you understand so that you can build up a basic picture of the subject. You will also need to consider whether or not you like a textbook. If you find it too difficult, then you are not ready for it. Start off at a level that you feel comfortable with and build towards more complex material as your reading skills and knowledge base develop. Never feel too proud to read a book aimed at a level of study you have passed – as long as it helps you to understand what you need to know. If you do not understand information, you cannot remember it and you cannot use it in different ways (Martin et al. 2010). Textbooks can evoke emotional responses in people; if you find the text too dense or the illustrations off-putting, you are less likely to use the book. If you don't like a textbook, try to find one that you do like.

To understand written information you will need to read sections of material and write down, in brief notes, what you think it means. You should then look at other sources of information to check your understanding and gain a deeper insight into that subject. Eventually, you will be able to write and talk about it quite confidently. Education is a process of increasing the depth, complexity and breadth of your knowledge, as well as developing your ability and confidence in your health and social care practice.

Although reading for writing is a necessary skill for you to develop, you may find other ways of understanding important concepts so that you can write about them. For example, your peers, practice mentor, lecturer or supervisor may discuss ideas with you and even suggest ways of making them easier to understand or read about. Reflecting on practice to identify your learning needs is a good way of breaking down the theory – practice gap (see Chapter 5) and will motivate you to want to learn more. It is important for you to articulate your understanding of ideas in order to build your knowledge. This is why informal activities, where you discuss a topic and maybe produce a hand-written poster or feed back to the group, are often built into your university programme delivery. Any group-work situation can be both a great learning opportunity and a potential distraction from the work. The more effort you put into it, the more you will gain from it. Where you have a choice of group-work colleagues, always look for those who will apply themselves to the task and maintain their focus on the task in hand. Choose them as group-work colleagues and you may well develop a mutual support network.

Where you are assigned to a group, show leadership and open the discussion about what the task entails, who will be responsible for each aspect of it, and how the group's time will be organised. If someone else takes a positive lead, show support for them and work towards the common goal. If the group is procrastinating, redirect your colleagues towards the task. If you feel that the group is not working, discuss it with the rest of the group. Become a good role model by applying yourself to the task and enjoying it. Ultimately, if others do not work, they are denying themselves a learning opportunity – do not be persuaded by peer pressure into doing the same. Remember, the more effort you put into the learning opportunities you are offered, the more you will learn and the better practitioner you will become. Your professional team-working skills to achieve goals in practice will be developed in this way. This is a situation where motivation and determination to achieve will reap rewards. If you are involved in working on a project over a longer period, you could try building rewards into group working, such as going out for a coffee afterwards. Wherever your inspiration comes from, jot down a few notes to remind you of your ideas so that when you sit down to write you are ready to start.

Feedback for success

Like any skill, writing is one that improves with practice and experience. You wouldn't expect to run a world-record marathon the first time you ran with a running club, so don't expect your writing to be brilliant straightaway. Just aim to do your best and make sure you check your writing for simple errors before submission. In writing, as with other skills, you need to learn from experience in order to improve. When you check the feedback on your work, if you just look at the mark and accept that as your level of achievement then you are unlikely to improve in the future. If you read the feedback carefully and make notes of what you need to do to write better in the future, then you will find it easier to progress. Tutorial feedback is particularly important, as it should guide you to improve the writing you are currently working on. Make sure you act on the feedback you are given. If you don't understand it, ask for clarification. Never be afraid to ask questions. In adult education, students are expected to seek out the support they need. This is true in both theory and practice settings.

Activity 2.6 Acting on feedback

Find feedback that you have been given either on the piece you are currently writing or on similar pieces that you have written previously. List below the key points that you will need to consider in order to improve your writing:

-
-
-
-
-
-

Keep a copy of this list with your current writing project and update it every time you are given feedback.

Accessing learning support

Universities fund learning support services for all students. Not everyone has been able to acquire all the study skills needed for higher education in the course of their pre-university experience. To ensure that students are not disadvantaged by this, universities often offer regular sessions about different aspects of studying, such as academic writing, referencing, note making and accessing literature. They will often have written or electronic guides to support study skills as well. Have a look for learning support services on your university intranet. You'll probably find there is a lot more help than you realised. It is strongly advisable to access all open study skills sessions or lectures and guides, as even the most advanced student can benefit from refreshing their focus and enthusiasm for the process of studying and writing. Also, learning support services are familiar with current trends and new study aids, so an annual refresher is generally a good idea. Sometimes though, students may want to discuss their study skills with a qualified learning support tutor. Each university provides different services, but many have some appointments available for students who want to discuss how they might improve their study and writing skills. If you have any kind of writing block or fear of examinations or assignments, learning support tutors will usually be able to give you helpful advice for overcoming them. Sometimes lecturers may recommend that you see a learning support tutor because they think that the standard of your work (and therefore your marks) could be improved by working on your study skills. This might include time management, academic writing style, referencing, accessing appropriate literature or essay writing structure, for example. If this is the case, it is generally useful to take the feedback form and the assignment with you to your first appointment so that the learning support tutor can identify the key areas where you need support. Remember, a learning support tutor can only help you with your study skills. They cannot help you with the content of your work.

Some students have specific learning needs due to dyslexia or dyspraxia or because English is their second language. If you have, or think you may have, a specific learning need, you may need an assessment by an educational psychologist to identify your specific needs and how they may be met. For example, some students may be entitled to recording pens to transfer notes from lectures directly to a word-processing file. Do check with your lecturer before recording their lectures and remember that their lectures are intellectual property and cannot be published electronically or in hard copy. Some students may also be entitled to the loan of a university laptop with specialist software such as mind mapping to aid them with their studies. Some may need longer times in examinations or practical assessments. Those with dyspraxia may have difficulty with typing and practical skills. Again, they may require specific help with equipment, both for studying and for practice, and longer periods for examinations and practical assessments. Learning support tutors have specialist knowledge and experience, and if you have been assessed as having specific learning needs you are often eligible to one-to-one support from them. There will generally be at least one learning support tutor who specialises in working with students of health and social care and understands specific needs related to practice and can advise on strategies for managing specific situations: for example, administration of medicines; computerised record keeping and communication; reading and record writing; supporting service users to complete forms to access financial or other support.

If you speak English as a second language, learning support tutors will be able to advise you and your lecturers on your specific needs, and the university will often have dedicated web resources to aid your learning. For all students who have identified specific learning needs, the university has a responsibility to provide support on the basis of your specific assessment, so it is important that you access assessment and support as early as possible.

Conclusion

This chapter has identified some of the barriers to writing in health and social care, and strategies for overcoming them, including breaking down tasks into manageable pieces, maintaining a healthy work–life balance and rewarding writing behaviours. It has demonstrated the importance of writing in understanding the theory and practice of health and social care disciplines, as well as encouraging you to explore your own motivations for writing. It has identified the importance of having a place to write in, and suggested ways of making or finding a functional and pleasant writing environment. It has discussed getting started and finishing with points for your next writing session, in order to avoid the barrier to getting started again. It has identified the importance of accessing basic texts and research articles, as well as discussion and group work, to gain ideas for your writing about health and social care. Using feedback to improve your writing has been reviewed, and the purpose and importance of accessing learning support services generally, and particularly for specific learning needs, has been considered.

Hints and tips

- It is better to write something, even if you are not happy with it, than to write nothing – you can edit later.
- Be patient with yourself – writing is a skill that takes practice to improve.
- Believe in your own ability and keep trying.
- Spend time with people who want to write and study.
- Identify what you need to do and break it down into manageable tasks.

- When your motivation dips, read over your reasons for wanting to write.
- Reward yourself for every small achievement.
- Make or find your own writing space.
- Use textbooks that you like and understand.
- Use feedback to identify your writing needs.
- Access learning support for assessment and advice.
- Writing will help you to become a better health and social care professional.

References

Bandura, A. (1997) *Self-Efficacy: The Exercise of Control*. New York: Worth Publishers.

Bee, H. and Boyd, D. (2011) *The Developing Child*. Harlow: Pearson Education.

Buzan, T. (2011) *Buzan's Study Skills: Mind Maps, Memory Techniques, Speed Reading and More!* Harlow: BBC Active/Pearson.

Hayes, N. (2010) *Teach Yourself: Understand Psychology*. London: Hodder Education.

Martin, G. N., Carlson, N. R. and Buskist, W. (2010) *Psychology*. Harlow: Allyn & Bacon.

Michael, J. and Richardson, A. (2008) Healthcare for all: the independent inquiry into access to healthcare for people with learning disabilities, *Tizard Learning Disability Review*, 13(4): 28–34.

Nunez, R. and Freeman, W. J. (eds) (1999) *Reclaiming Cognitions: The Primacy of Action, Intention and Emotion*. Thorverton: Imprint Academic.

Paschler, H., McDaniel, M., Rohrer, D. and Bjork, R. (2008) Learning styles: concepts and evidence, *Psychological Science in the Public Interest, 9(3)*: 105–119.

3

Basic writing and essay planning skills

Julie Williams, Elizabeth Cooper and Amanda Clarke

This chapter explores the following topics:

- Writing for a purpose
- Demonstrating your learning through academic writing
- The rules of academic writing
- Demonstrating thinking through academic writing
- Essay writing
- Planning, writing and structuring the main body
- How to phrase your work: to quote or not to quote?
- Making the most of your conclusion
- Using feedback to improve your writing

Introduction

This chapter begins by looking at why you write and for what purpose. By understanding how to use your writing skills effectively you will be able to demonstrate your knowledge and communicate what you need to say, or report, in a concise way that conveys your message clearly. This chapter will guide you through how to learn these skills and use them through the medium of essay writing as an example. The chapter will also help you to structure your thoughts, set out your intentions and formulate a plan. We discuss how to make the best use of the words you choose and how using the correct grammar can enhance your writing. This will help you construct written reports which are professionally meaningful and academic assignments which meet the required learning outcomes. The chapter will guide you through how to understand what an assignment task is asking from you and how best to organise your thoughts for the necessary reading and note taking you need to do in preparation for planning an essay. This planning is important. Therefore we offer some suggestions for how to use mind mapping effectively. In addition, we provide some helpful tips on structuring your writing, introducing your work, signposting your intentions and making a clear and effective argument, all within the word limit of the assignment task. Practical tips are provided on the appropriate use of common grammatical conventions, use of quotations and how to round off your writing by making the most of your conclusion. Finally, this chapter helps you to use feedback to improve your writing 'for learning' and 'of learning', making the most of every available opportunity from multiple sources, including finding and using 'critical friends'.

Writing, in any language, is a key part of communication. Whatever we write, it always serves a purpose and is written for a specific audience. You write a shopping list to help you remember to buy everything; letter writing expresses your intentions. Writing for academic reasons is no different. For university students there are several reasons why you need to write whilst studying at university, but without exception the writer (you) must know the intended audience. In this world the audience is the academic community.

Writing for a purpose

Achieving competence in writing is essential to academic success. However, for students of professional health and social care education programmes there are additional purposes to writing whilst undertaking graduate studies. A key objective is to prepare students to work with other professionally qualified graduates in professions where making decisions, giving a rationale for actions (being accountable) and sharing ideas with colleagues are daily occurrences. In addition, communicating with professional regulators, professional bodies, and/or working at local, national or international levels means that competent writing skills demonstrate high standards of professional practice. In this way writing competently is essential for professional working throughout all health and social care services, for exemplifying professional accountability, and to clearly show logical and critical debate underpinning all decisions.

Academic writing is the basis of an internationally understood term for writing at university level where members of the academic community need to understand each other. To do this, specific conventions need to be used. Therefore a key element for achieving success in writing tasks within the academic community is for students is to learn the basic elements of this code of conventions. A common approach to developing these skills is to require students to complete different writing tasks for differentiated audiences and with increasing complexity as their studies advance. Coupled with the requirement to demonstrate preparedness for the real world of working practices in health and social care services, students are increasingly being encouraged to publish their work and a number of mechanisms exist to facilitate this. However, by far the most frequent type of academic writing that university students are required to do is in the format of an essay.

Demonstrating your learning through academic writing

The main aim of submitting work is for you to demonstrate to your lecturer what you have learnt. In particular your learning should demonstrate knowledge, understanding and application to the topic. One of the most difficult things you will need to do is manage the amount of learning materials you have with what materials will be excluded from your essay.

As you become more involved in preparing, planning and thinking about your writing task, being able to judge if your final written version meets the assignment submission requirements can be very challenging and anxiety inducing. Gaining feedback from other sources should be considered as a necessary part of developing your presentation and academic writing skills. To help you structure your thoughts it may be helpful to think of the knowledge you have gained as 'bricks', which are not particularly useful in isolation but if constructed together will eventually provide a useful 'whole'. In planning any academic writing, analysing and interpreting the evidence you have read will enable you to use these chunks of knowledge in ways that enable you to construct an argument and formulate an effective written piece of work. In this way your thought processes will be the 'mortar' that holds these chunks (bricks) together.

As well as getting your thinking right, being able to present your work in a way that makes reading and therefore marking easier is an important skill. This again can be planned for, but there are general 'rules' for presentation in academic style which we can now go on to discuss.

The rules of academic writing

Tone and vocabulary

Academic writing is difficult to define. Even within the term 'academic writing' there is large variation between both subject area and level. There are many different ways of writing academically, but they all have the one common thread: Standard English. Standard English dictates the tone of academic work as writing in a formal way about a situation and includes using correct punctuation, grammar and sentencing to get a clear message across. All writers adopt different styles but all conform to the rules of Standard English as regards sentence construction, punctuation, grammar, spelling and vocabulary (Open University 2003).

In contrast to spoken words, standard written English aims to use an internationally agreed format using words, rather than colloquial, or spoken, dialect. It is therefore useful to think of Standard English as an almost exclusively written dialect. It is a way of writing that can be learned and due to its international appeal it enables you, as a university student, to communicate effectively with people in the academic environment. Once learned, and a level of success has been achieved, you will be able to write fluently and thus increase your chances of academic success in your career.

Tips for Standard English

- Avoid use of 'I', 'we' and 'they'; use non-personal wording.
- Use of the first person is acceptable when writing reflectively: for example, 'I experienced a deeper understanding of the processes involved as a result of my experience.'
- Do not use slang: for example, 'The use of personal protective equipment such as a *pinny* [apron] was. . . .'

- Avoid abbreviations unless they are commonly used within your field of work: for example, 'The National Health Service [NHS] was established. . . .'
- Do not list words or number your points. Write full sentences, using colons, semi-colons or commas – see examples later in this chapter.

Activity 3.1 Writing in Standard English

The following are examples of colloquial speech, that is, non-standard English. See if you can 'translate' them into Standard English before reading the translations provided.

Colloquial speech: 'They usually only do their exercises after you make them a bit of a laugh and joke. It's dead sweet, but frustrating at times', said Mary.

Suggested Standard English 'translation': Mary believes that patients become interested in their physiotherapy treatment only because of its comedy value. She finds this very frustrating but quite endearing.

Note the use of the third person to report Mary's opinion, for example: 'Mary believes'.

Now you try a 'translation':

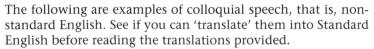

Colloquial speech: 'Her evening 8pm observations are well dodgy.'
Your translation would be:

_____

_____

_____

_____

Suggested Standard English 'translation': Upon comparison with the patients initial baseline physiological measurements, the results of the evening measurements at eight pm were found to be worthy of further investigation.

Note the use of the written number as opposed to the numerical number in the colloquial speech. It is usual to write the number in full if it is a single figure.

Structuring sentences: the basics

Collins Concise Dictionary defines a sentence as: 'A sequence of words capable of standing alone to make an assertion, ask a question or give a command, usually consisting of a subject and a predicate' (Collins 2009). This definition makes it clear that a sentence must be 'capable of standing alone'. Reading your work out loud should enable you to identify phrases that do not stand alone; they will sound peculiar.

The sentence is the building block of good writing and can be short, long, complicated or simple. However, they all:

- begin with a capital letter
- end with a full stop
- need two things: a subject and a verb.

Examples of 'subjects' could be: *rain, person, boat*. Examples of 'verbs' could be: *to drop, to walk, to snore, to stop*. If we combine these elements, we make sentences:

Sentence = subject + verb.

Therefore: The rain dropped. A person snores. The boat stops.

Sentences may also contain an object, such as: The rain dropped on *her*. A person snores in *bed*. The boat stops at the *buoy*. In this way the object of the sentence has something done *to it*. The object often follows the verb (the action word):

Sentence = subject + verb + object.

Adding another object: The rain dropped on her in the *courtyard*. A person snores in bed when at *home*. The boat stops at the buoy in the *harbour*:

Sentence = subject + verb + object + indirect object.

You can also give more detail about the subject or object. For example: The *heavy* rain dropped on her in the *public* courtyard. An *overweight* person snores in bed when at his *holiday* home. The *new* boat stops at the buoy in the *nearest* harbour:

Sentence = description + subject + verb + object + description
+ indirect object.

Prepositions are used to join words which link the different parts of these sentences together. Word such as: *to, at, before, between, above, over, on, in, with, without, during, under.* They add to the communicative clarity of the sentence.

Sentences are the core component of paragraphs. Paragraphs are blocks of text, longer than one sentence, that explain one point or argument within the main content of your essay. Without paragraphs, your work appears very long and it can be difficult for the reader to make sense of the arguments you are trying to articulate. Ensure that you identify paragraphs clearly by starting them on a new line. You can present this clearly by either starting the paragraph with a 'hanging indent', i.e. stepped in, or by leaving an extra 'line space' between each. Check with your programme leader which style is acceptable to your university.

Tips for getting sentencing right!

- To improve the clarity of what you have noted, speak the words out loud. Repeat this a few times until the message is clear. This will help you to identify if you are unclear or waffling.
- Use fewer words wherever possible and keep sentences short.
- To achieve a good sentence length, read it out loud and where you naturally take a breath consider using grammar to support sentence construction.
- Correctly using full stops, commas, semi-colons and colons will ensure sentences make sense.

Passive style

The preferred tone within academic writing is a passive style, meaning that the subject of the sentence has something done to it. Using a passive style develops a more detached and formal tone to your writing. This tone implies to a reader that the writer has thought about the information they are relaying. Presenting your writing using the passive style helps you to demonstrate your thinking and consideration of key information. This again helps to improve your communication to the reader and increase your potential to attract marks.

Activity 3.2 Using the passive style

Active: He made the pancakes.   **Passive:** The pancakes were made by him.

Active: Ellie wrote the speech.   **Passive:** The speech was written by Ellie.

As you can see, using the passive voice gives a detached and formal feel to your writing. Now you try:

Active: The dog ate the slipper.

Passive: . . . .

Active: Mary wrote the exam papers.

Passive: . . . .

Being precise will pay dividends

When writing it is important that you do not let your thoughts wander. Say what you mean and mean what you say to avoid any confusion of thought and prose. Always use words sparingly and appropriate to your task and do not use unnecessary padding out of sentences (verbiage). Generally, all your written assignments will be restricted to a predetermined word limit. Therefore learning to write clearly and convey a clear message in as few words as possible is an important writing skill. Simply, using fewer words of higher quality will increase your rate of success.

In health and social care education and practice there is a requirement to learn, develop and include specialist language and vocabulary in writing tasks in a meaningful way. You will no doubt initially be overwhelmed by the proliferation of specialist language and vocabulary when you first start your health and/or social care programmes of study, but actively listening to lecturers, experts, clients, patients and other professionals alike will help you to familiarise yourself with the language until you reach the point of feeling comfortable enough to use it effectively yourself. Accessing online or purchasing a professional dictionary should be something you do early on in your educational programme and will help you to effectively use a range of vocabulary throughout your professional career. Using an online thesaurus can also be invaluable in writing assignments.

If English is not your first language, it is strongly recommended that you access all the available assistance each university will provide. This can be particularly important when you are not only required to write in an unfamiliar language but also tasked with learning a specialist vocabulary. All forms of feedback will be invaluable to you and will enhance your success.

Tips for improving academic tone

- Avoid the bad habit of using language that can be considered as slang, text speak or incomprehensible abbreviations: for example, nah instead of no; L8R instead of later, I not i.
- Avoid words used as local dialect: for example, och aay instead of yes; innit instead of isn't it?
- Avoid use of contractions: for example, it's should be written as it is; don't should be written as do not; you've should be written as you have; can't should be written as cannot.
- Always write the number in full if it is a single figure.

Activity 3.3 Precision: plain and simple

> Obfuscation, ambiguity, lack of clarity, waffle and other things can lead to the central idea getting lost in irrelevant, unnecessary and extraneous detail that is of no consequence, account or relevance to the central tenet or thesis of what it is that you are actually attempting to communicate or get across to those people who may cast their eyes across the fruits of your academic efforts.
>
> (Hurley 2012: 16)

As you can see almost all of these words fail to make sense of what the writer is attempting to convey. Try to rewrite the sentence so that it makes sense in a concise way:

_____

_____

_____

_____

_____

_____

Using the comma

The comma, if used properly, can enhance the clarity of your writing. Examine the following sentences:

Ellie spun around a baton in her hand.

Ellie spun around, a baton in her hand.

You can see from the two sentences above that where the comma has been placed completely changes the emphasis and meaning of the sentence. You may be able to determine where a comma is required by reading out loud; thus it can be a useful technique although not entirely guaranteed of success on every occasion.

A note of caution: overusing the comma, however subtle, may negatively affect your writing style (King 2000; Trask 2000). Too many commas can ruin a sentence:

Generally, although, not explicitly, Mrs Roberts bought from NASDA, the supermarket, the ingredients for her cake baking, including flour, sultanas, butter and, sugar, every Saturday, unless, fortuitously, her daughter went for her.

(13 commas)

Corrected version:

Generally, although not explicitly, Mrs Roberts bought from NASDA the supermarket the ingredients for her cake baking, including flour, sultanas, butter and sugar every Saturday unless, fortuitously, her daughter went for her.

(7 commas)

Difficulties in tone and style of academic writing

As with all forms of academic writing, there are certain common problems to be aware of. In Table 3.1 we identify some problems and their solutions.

Demonstrating thinking through academic writing

Standard English is not the only important characteristic of academic writing: To be effective your writing must have structure and contain a logical argument, or at least a reasoned claim. Such claims must

Table 3.1 Problems in academic writing

Problem	Solution
Long sentences	Use sentences that make a point; deal with one main point per sentence.
Sentences which try to cover several points	Each sentence and paragraph should depict one main but precise purpose.
Verbiage (unnecessary 'padding out' of sentences), commonly known as 'waffle'	Excessive use of words will over-complicate your writing and may cause confusion at best and misinterpretation at worst. Use words sparingly to reflect meaning. This can take several attempts or edits. Rewriting things so they are punchier is an important skill.
Lack of direction	Be clear about what you want to say in your writing. Use signposts and subheadings if they help clarify what you are trying to say.
Over formality	Use simple words that say what they mean. For example, why say 'writing implement' when 'pen' would work just as well? However, do not make the mistake of nullifying field-specific language or accepted professionally related dialect.

(Plain-English-Campaign 2012)

be clearly presented and supported with relevant information and/ or evidence, in a logical way. This includes being able to critically analyse the issue, identify omissions and/or inconsistencies and by articulating a balanced argument. In this way you will be able to formulate a coherent picture using the written word, of the issue you wish to convey. You will be assessed on your ability to substantiate your claims by the careful and judicious use of credible reference sources.

Academic writing is more than just writing about what you have read. Your lecturers are not solely interested in the content of what you have read or how much time you have spent avoiding the library. The concern here is more to do with your ability to demonstrate, in writing, the results and learning gained from the time you have spent reading. Your reasoning and the rationale for your views and opinions should therefore be adequately supported by robust research evidence.

Throughout your programme of study your thoughts, interpretations and critical analysis about your subject matter will mature and progress. You will come to internalise many key features of your subject and gain a deeper level of understanding so your knowledge will increase at each distinguishable academic level and all the way through your programme of study. In this way critical thinking is demonstrated throughout your degree programme to increasing levels of sophistication and competence.

Academic endeavours at university relate to a number of key words used to identify the level, style and approach needed within a written task. These are linked to an academic level of thinking and achievement and are universally applied. You can also read more about this in Chapter 4.

Further understanding of these different levels of academic writing whilst studying at university can be found at www.businessballs. com/bloomstaxonomyoflearningdomains.htm

---

To validate your thinking and progressing knowledge about your subject your academic writing needs to demonstrate year-on-year improvement. At the beginning of your studies you will be asked to write about the literature you have read, known as *descriptive writing*. The limitations of this level of writing reside in the 'reporting' of what you have read, because there is not much thinking involved in descriptive writing. In Chapter 4, you can read more about descriptive writing and other levels of academic writing.

Reviewing your skills

You have now worked through several aspects of academic writing which are concerned with the presentation of your work. If you are new to academic writing or are progressing through your programmes, you need to be and remain 'skilled' in academic writing. As with any skill, practice and seeking expert help can keep you at your best and will continue to improve all aspects of your academic writing. It is also important, and perhaps reassuring, to note that many students only discover that they have a degree of dyslexia or other learning disability once they need to write for their degree.

This may require specialist support and the earlier you recognise that you require help the better chance of increasing your success in your assessment tasks. Together you can use a structured approach to assess your writing skills that can help to locate your individual strengths and areas for further development, which may require additional support.

Once you have completed some assignment and writing tasks at university you will receive feedback. This should be in a written format for you to keep. You should carefully review your feedback from each and every piece of work, especially if you have failed. At the end of each assessment period you, and perhaps your personal academic tutor, should be planning to improve your academic writing and how to progress to the next academic level.

Tips for reviewing your writing skills

- What feedback and advice have I had relating to my use of English or tone?
- What feedback and advice have I had from previous work relating to my use of sentences and grammar?
- Do I know where to go for writing support in the university?
- I'm not sure where to ask for help? *Answer*: see your personal academic tutor.

Now you have explored your academic writing skills, we move on to actually writing the essay!

Essay writing

Essay assignments will usually contribute to a significant number of summative assessments that you will be required to undertake for your health and social care degree. There are several stages to writing an essay that the following sections will take you through: understanding the task; the starter plan; writing your introduction; planning, writing and structuring the main body; and making the most of your conclusions. By following these stages and starting early you can prevent some common errors relating to an assignment: for example, late submission (where your marks are penalised) or poor presentation (losing easy marks!). In ensuring you work in a logical fashion such as presented in the next part of the chapter, you can avoid these pitfalls and improve your marks.

We will look at the essay in particular as this remains one the most popular assignment tasks, although it may also go under the titles of: commentary, report, reflection (where a framework may be stipulated), patchwork text, to name but a few. All of these types of assignment will need to follow the core structure requirements by containing the sections of introduction, main body and conclusion. Using these sections helps in ensuring a clear, logical, systematic structure to your work, providing a very effective way of showing your lecturer the knowledge you have gained, your level of under-standing and how you have applied this to certain situations or examples. Remember, it is not what you know, but what you do with it that counts.

You do not have to write your essay in order. Some people find it better to write their introduction at the end, when they know what the essay contains. However you tackle your essay, the end product needs to have the three main structural elements easily identified.

Note taking and preparing to plan

Read your materials and literature to collect your thoughts and note what you think they are telling you. Avoid copying down the information verbatim; in this way you are already displaying your initial interpretations and thoughts. Themes, propositions and argument development will become more apparent as you accrue more information and start to make sense of it. Keeping your notes electronically may help you to be – and stay – organised. Following a planning process, which is presented later in this chapter, makes it easier for you to see exactly what you need to know and what to leave out in order to construct your answer. In this way any gaps in your knowledge will also become apparent and will enable you to refine your thoughts and ideas so that you can achieve a high level of precision in your work. There are sev-eral ways to develop a plan for your writing task that will enable you to have a clear, logical flow to your work. The structure of any writing task needs to make the hard hours of thinking and study-ing appear easy.

Essay titles or tasks are often expressed as a statement or a ques-tion that needs addressing and your essay should be a personal dem-onstration of the knowledge and thoughts relating to this title or task. Do not underestimate how valuable is the time spent thinking, planning and reading in relation to your writing task and how it will benefit the final piece of work. Good planning will help you bring together all the skills you will use to produce a good piece of academic writing. So, to start you need to ensure you understand what you are expected to do.

Decoding the assessment task

Essay titles or tasks can be simple, varied, complex and/or in multiple parts. No matter how the task is presented, it generally depicts a question that must be addressed in the main body of the essay. Getting started requires understanding the task and planning your initial work. The following box gives some examples of key 'directive' or 'instructive' words that commonly appear in essay titles, with some explanations. These are not exhaustive.

Understanding what needs doing – academic writing verbs

- **Analyse** Divide and examine each component part.
- **Compare** Look for similarities and differences between each aspect.
- **Contrast** Explore opposite elements to identify differences.
- **Critique** Highlight strengths and weaknesses of each discussion point.
- **Define** Set down the precise meaning of a word or phrase.
- **Describe** Give a detailed descriptive account.
- **Discuss** Examine by argument, giving pros and cons.
- **Evaluate** Appraise the worth of something; include your personal opinion.
- **Examine** Carefully consider the depth and implications of an issue.
- **Explain** To interpret and account for.
- **Interpret** Make clear/explicit the meaning; provide evidence of own judgements.
- **Outline** Give the main features of a subject, omitting minor details.
- **Review** Examine the subject critically.
- **Summarise** A concise account of the chief points, omitting details and examples.

Tips for understanding the task

- Break down each aspect of the task to identify key words, components or sections/parts.
- Every part *must* then be answered.
- Use a dictionary or thesaurus to look for alternative explanations of essay titles.

Here are two exercises for you to attempt which will help you practise breaking down some essay titles and tasks. You should also spend time thinking about where and how you would start your essay, if you were to write it.

Activity 3.4 Unpicking an essay title

For each of the example essay titles given below underline the key words and interpret what the question is actually asking you to do.

Essay titles:

- Explain the terms 'ethics' and 'accountability' as they relate to nursing practice.
- Analyse the different learning styles that may be utilised when learning new skills.
- Examine how the nurse's role can contribute to the development of a healthy community.
- Critically discuss intrinsic and extrinsic motivation as it relates to nursing leadership.

Activity 3.5 Complex essay title

In this hypothetical recent publication *Getting a Degree without Writing An Essay*, U. R. Deadold and N. O. Insight (2002) argue that writing essays at university is a complete waste of time. To what extent do you agree with this point of view?

How would you begin to answer this question?

_____

_____

_____

_____

_____

Starter plan: using mind mapping

Mind maps are tools that help you to organise your thoughts and learning by writing down the central core idea and thinking up new and related ideas which connect to this central idea. They help you to summarise your knowledge and build up a picture of all aspects of the question that need to be addressed. The use of lines, colours, arrows or branches will show relationships between your ideas. Such techniques promote linear thinking, helping you to see how your ideas (or arguments) have developed. They can also help you 'make connections' between areas, helping with your creative thinking.

The mind mapping technique is a dynamic process that can be added to over time in preparation for drafting a more structured essay plan. A comprehensive mind map is useful in two distinct but equally valuable ways. It can be used for helping to plan an essay and as a guide (Option A). You start off with your assessment task and key words and identify the initial areas you want to investigate. To begin with you should mark down everything you know about the essay subject. Explore all aspects and attempt to draw relationships between key areas by drawing your first lines and identifying questions to explore. As you review and add to the map, you can add another set of 'lines' layers, or develop smaller 'maps' of the new ideas, thoughts or topics you have found (Option B). In Activity 3.6 you have the opportunity to draw an initial mind map plan.

Tip for getting started

You can get useful information for this initial mind map when your tutor/lecturer launches or goes over the assessment requirements. This is when you are being directed to things that you should begin looking at for your essays.

Activity 3.6 Mapping from a title: 'Explore the ethical concepts that underpin nursing practice'

Initial mind map

So, after completing the initial mind map you can use one of the two options:

- *Option A*: use this to plan the essay, adding on lines for where to look for further questions to explore.
- *Option B*: use this to add any ideas/thoughts/questions that have been identified and raised building upon essay 'content' and direction.

For level four academic work where descriptive writing is required, Option A would be adequate. For higher levels, where arguments are needed (levels 5 and 6), or 'creative' linking of ideas or theories (levels 6 and 7), Option B would be more useful. You should practise using Option A as this will enable you to become confident in the use of mind maps, and provide you with a guide for your own thinking whilst planning the essay. Mind maps can also be very useful as an aide memoire. At higher levels of academic writing, undertaking a mind mapping exercise can allow time for you to 'think' about what you have read or found out, and make connections about the information you have discovered. This is critically important for writing a clear and well-structured essay.

Tips for using mind maps

- Use your mind map as the initial key words for searching databases and libraries.
- Use 'topic titles' from your mind map in an electronic library such as Endnote.
- Keep all your information together, showing linkages and connections.
- As you develop ideas from your initial read (and complete your next mind map), repeat the scan read. This focuses your reading and ensures you can read a higher volume of relevant information.

Introducing and signposting your essay

The essay introduction is the heartbeat that puts the piece of work into context. It provides clarity of purpose and direction for the reader. The introduction puts the question into context and gives the reader a clear indication of the direction the answer will take. By assisting the reader (and marker) you are demonstrating a logical and systematic approach, which are key requirements for communicating your knowledge and understanding within an essay. Signposting is one of the key tasks you do when essay writing, as it can clearly identify how the essay is structured. There are some useful signposting words that are acceptable and useful in academic writing. Using these words, as part of your sentencing, provides a 'map' for the reader to your work. Examples of 'signpost' words have been italicised in an example below to illustrate how this works.

Example

Let us imagine that you have been given this essay question:
'Critically evaluate and analyse the political, social and personal impact of the transition of care from child to adult mental health services in the UK'

An introduction may read as follows:

This assignment will *provide a critical account* of the transition from Child and Adolescent Mental Health Services (CAMHS) to Adult Mental Health Services (AMHS). A *critique* of the literature will contextualise the rationale for choosing the subject and its relevance to current practice. It will *discuss* relevant Government policies and how the two services take very different approaches to care provision. Importantly it will include *a review of the barriers* facing service users' transitions between services, the potential *influences of family* and the *transferability of nursing skills* between CAMHS and AMHS staff. The *complexity* of transferring from a service that provides a familiar, established routine, as experienced by children over a number of years whilst a service user of CAMHS to an unfamiliar and new routine in AMHS, stimulated a keen interest in developing an understanding of the personal impact of these changes. Further catalysts for choosing the topic include *a desire to understand the context of Government polices* (DCSF, 2007; DCSF, 2009b; DCSF, 2010b) and the immediate *personal impact* these may have at an individual service user and family level, as well as the potential to affect staff both personally, professionally and developmentally. This *review aims to explore* the transition between services and the influences of different patterns of provision and the level of support service users may receive. It would seem that this may impact on their levels of service user compliance and/or disempowerment including the effect on families and individual autonomy.

Once you move into the main body of your essay argument you may find it helpful to start and end each paragraph with a signpost phrase. The boxed words and phrases are useful signposts.

In keeping with A's (date) statement that . . .
It could be argued that . . .
On the other hand
The logical conclusion would be
Unlike Deadold and Insight (2002), Modernman (2012) states that . . .
While both Deadold and Insight (2002), and Modernman (2012) agree that . . . , only Modernman (2012) states that . . .
On the contrary; Conversely

Firstly, secondly, thirdly, Finally
While Deadold and Insight (2002) are of the opinion that . . . ,
  Modernman (2012) believes . . .
In addition; Simultaneously, concurrently
After, afterwards, after this
Subsequently; Following this, As a result of
Therefore, Hence
For this reason
Following this line of argument
Given B's (date) opinion that . . .
Thus, it becomes evident that . . .
Similarly
In the same way, It follows that
But; then; next; yet; however
Nevertheless; because; consequently
Despite; though
If we take Modernman's (2012) view to be correct . . .

Activity 3.7 Writing a good introduction

Look at the following two introductions. In this hypothetical recent publication *Getting a Degree without Writing An Essay*, U. R. Deadold and N. O. Insight (2002) argue that writing essays at university is a complete waste of time. To what extent do you agree with this point of view?

1 When I read Deadold and Insight's book I got a really bad feeling they were setting out to upset all students. Being a student is hard enough without anyone suggesting it is easy. I often get upset by the marks I get because I spend ages reading loads of boring books and I didn't really understand what Deadold was getting at so I will just include everything in the following essay and hope for the best and I am hoping that by reading what Deadold said I can make an argument so that I don't get disappointed because I can see where everything can get mixed up with everything else that I wrote.

In this hypothetical recent publication *Getting a Degree without Writing An Essay*, U. R. Deadold and N. O. Insight (2002) argue that writing essays at university is a complete waste of time. To what extent do you agree with this point of view?

2 Deadold and Insight (2002) have written extensively about the negative impact of studying at university and the prolific use of essay writing as a means of summative assessment. However, their views, often based on opinion and not empirical evidence, tend to be rather extreme and in direct conflict with established authors in this field. It can be argued that the effectiveness of other assessment methods within the context of higher education are comparable to the essay but it is not yet established that the essay has limited value as a means of summative assessment. This paper will aim to demonstrate the utility of the essay as a mean of assessment and the intrinsic value it has when used in the appropriate manner.

Can you identify what would be considered the better introduction from these two examples? Use the information on presentation and 'signposting' principles when reading the examples.

Tips for a good introduction

- Specifically mention what topics in relation to the title you are going to include.
- Give a brief 'tour' of the essay in the same order.
- Include some explanations of how you have considered the title; for example, by using a mind map to identify the main discussion/argument of your essay.
- Briefly explain how you deconstructed the task; for example, by underlining the key signposting words in the assessment brief.
- Include a selection of signposting words.
- Consider writing your introduction last to ensure it truly and accurately reflects your content.
- Ensure you adhere to the rules of academic writing.
- Make no spelling or grammatical errors as this is where you make your first impression on the marker. Make it good!

Planning, writing and structuring the main body

Using your initial plan and mind map as a guide, you now need to consider the main body of your essay. This involves identifying the depth and breadth of the argument to be made. Academic depth requires evidence of analysis, critical thinking and creative ideas within the writing (see Chapter 4 for a more detailed discussion). To plan for this depth, you'll need to use other techniques for capturing your ideas and recording the arguments you have considered. This may include the use of diagrams to help you plan your content. These diagrams can also provide an indication on the paragraphs, subsections or chapters you will need for your essay, which will enhance the structure of your main body. Here are two examples of different types of diagram that you can use to help you plan your essay and develop and decide on your argument and answer to the question set.

Example 1: Balancing an argument using scales

A 'scale' diagram such as the one demonstrated below can help you identify the different arguments you may want to consider for your essay.

'Essays are a waste of time by Deadold and Insight (2002)'

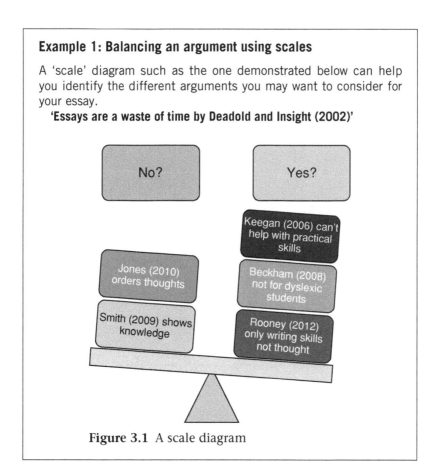

Figure 3.1 A scale diagram

Deadold and Insight (2002) hypothetical publication *Getting a Degree without Writing An Essay*, U. R. Deadold and N. O. Insight (2002). In this publication the authors argue that writing essays at university is a complete waste of time. Example 2 demonstrates the breadth of thoughts that could potentially form the basis of the essay answer.

Example 2: Managing and recording your flow of creative ideas and thoughts using a spider diagram

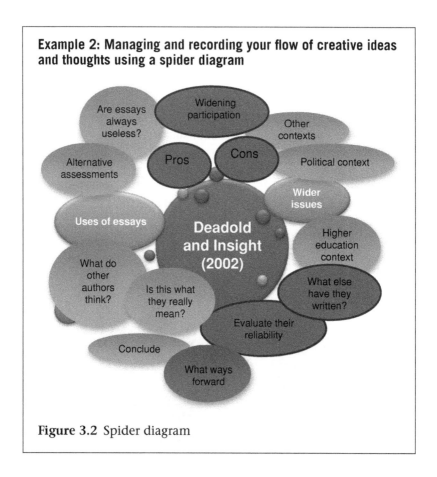

Figure 3.2 Spider diagram

Remember that this section of the essay is where the reader wants to find the answers to the task set by the essay question. Using diagrams to help you establish the different arguments to include in your essay will help you ensure that you succeed in doing so.

Working out the wordage

In getting the content of your main body clearer you need to know the amount of words you are expected to write for each aspect of the topic. Most essays have a specified work count as this makes the anticipated content the same for all. It can also provide a challenge if you feel you have a lot to say and not enough words. You should expect to write more than your 'expected' wordage in the planning stages and factor in some time for editing down the wordage to meet the word count. If you have the opportunity to get some feedback on draft work then use this to refine and revise your work.

How to phrase your work: to quote or not to quote?

Although it could be argued that phrasing your written work should be discussed in the section on academic style, it has been included here to emphasise the importance of acknowledging your sources within your main body of the essay. The 'flow' of your work becomes vitally important and finding balance between the articulation and use of your ideas with acknowledging facts and research evidence from other people is essential. Verbatim use of the printed word, known as quoting, is used by the writer judiciously as it can hinder the natural flow of their written text. Original written sources usually have their own unique style which is usually very different from your own writing, thus making it difficult to 'slip' in a quote without careful signposting. Having to 'break off' from your own writing to include a quote can be distracting for you and also for the reader/marker.

In some instances the quotes you use will be illustrative. This means that the quote does not directly state facts or an opinion but implies a similar message. In this instance quotes are used as a metaphor and can be really helpful in conveying to the reader your ideas in another way, for example, quoting from books, poetry and/or song lyrics. A word of caution: avoid using a string of quotes to 'pad out' your essay. It demonstrates very poor academic writing competence and will attract a negative response from your lecturers.

When you are tempted to put in a quote consider the following questions:

- Will the quotation add to your essay?
- Is it necessary?

- Will it improve what I am trying to say?
- Will paraphrasing distort the key messages of the material?
- Why will the quote say it better than me?
- Can I find the accurate reference, including the page number the words are from?

One valuable use of quotes is when referring to the use of seminal work. Seminal work is original work that is now accepted as fact: for example, Einstein's theory of relativity; Freud's psychoanalytic theory; Henderson's theory of nursing, to name but a few.

Your choice of use of natural language and direct quotes can be organised into your content plan. This plan illustrates where your topics are to be placed within the body of the essay and how they would fit together. The content plan helps you to structure your essay and map out your subsections and paragraphs by each one containing a separate aspect of your topic or argument. This then allows you to build up your argument and develop a logical and flowing piece of academic writing.

Making the most of your conclusion

The final part of your essay is your conclusion. This is your last chance to make that all-important impression. Therefore it should be relevant and constructed for all the right reasons. Your conclusion should be effectively signposted: i.e. To conclude this essay. . . . To summarise and bring my essay to an end . . . .

Making a good final impression requires as much detail, accuracy and phrasing as the rest of your essay. Usual academic conventions require conclusions to include a summation of your premises and a pulling together of all your arguments. In this way you will be able to demonstrate that the essay question has been answered and thus achieve a sense of closure for your essay. There should be a level of consistency between the introduction and the conclusions and no new topics, themes or material introduced. It should leave your reader in no doubt as to what you set out to do. Although most writers consider the conclusion the easiest part to write, this can be mistaken assumption.

Tips for your conclusion

- Avoid adding new information, no matter how interesting.
- Should not be more than ten per cent of your total essay wordage.
- Should be well written, making a strong lasting impression.
- Should confirm your main statements.
- Should remind the reader of the task you are answering.

Using feedback to improve your writing

Receiving other people's opinions about your work can improve your performance in academic and essay writing (Juwah et al. 2004; Brookhart 2008). Using feedback on draft work, where permissible, will enhance your final product and help you improve for subsequent assignments. Using feedback in this way aims to contribute to your learning in a number of ways. There are two types of feedback:

- For learning: where you gain advice on how to improve your work.
- Of learning: where your work is judged and given a 'mark'.

You can get feedback from many sources. However, it is important that you identify what you want from the person giving you the feedback so that you can make the most of the process. As well as feedback you may also be given some direction for future improvement which is termed 'feed-forward'. However, getting feedback does not mean asking someone to correct your work, rewrite your work, or fill in the gaps you cannot complete. All this would actually be classified as cheating.

Make the most of opportunities that the university provides for you such as tutorials, reviews of draft work, student support, study skills and personal development weeks. When accessing such support you should prepare questions to which you need answers before you attend; write them down so you remember to get a response. In this way you are making sure the feedback is relevant and pertinent to the areas in your work you are worried about.

Peer feedback is when other students help in developing learning through group tutorials, study groups and study buddy schemes, where students listen to each other's opinions to improve their own ideas (Brookhart 2008). A further useful method of getting reliable feedback is by asking a critical friend. This involves identifying an individual who does not know the content or ideas you have written about but who can knowledgably critique your work before it is submitted. They can provide an invaluable critical read-through and examine the essay for standards of presentation, structure and 'flow' of your written work. They do not necessarily need to know your topic but should have knowledge and competence in the use of Standard English, grammar, sentencing and language. They can give you invaluable feedback on whether your statements/arguments are clear and logical, whether they make sense, and confirm if you have answered the question and/or stuck to your intended plan.

Tips for getting feedback

Use some or all of these questions to improve the feedback you receive.
  For lecturers, does the essay:

- answer the question?
- have an introduction, main body and conclusion?
- contain relevant topics?
- include critical analysis of the claims/argument claim or argument?
- cite references accurately at all times, using the preferred referencing format?

For peers/critical friend, does the essay:

- use correct grammar, spelling and punctuation and the right word for the job?
- use appropriate and relevant information with supporting evidence?
- use an appropriate font, size and word processing package?
- use Standard English?
- avoid the use of contractions, slang or colloquialism?
- follow a logical structure?
- use sentences and paragraphs correctly?
- require a proofread?

Essay planner

As a final aide we provide a checklist for you to use so that you can assess your preparedness for academic writing and essay production.

Table 3.2 Essay planner

Key task	Where am I up to?	Action: what can I do to improve this aspect?
Translate the question into your own words.		
Read only what will help you answer the question.		
Access peer reviewed journals and consider lecture notes and websites as well as books.		
Use a range of language and vocabulary.		
Create plans to see how topics relate to the question.		
Can I use the preferred referencing style?		
Do I pay attention to grammatical detail?		
Do I have enough time for draft and redraft?		

In Table 3.2 we have identified some key tasks involved in essay planning and writing. For each task you should honestly assess where you are at and identify an activity to help you improve in each area. The table can be photocopied for use when starting an essay.

Conclusion

Improving your skills in academic writing and essay production takes time, patience, determination and practice. Some people have a natural ability when it comes to essay writing but even this will need nurturing to ensure there is improvement during your academic programme. Just as you are learning the topics for your degree, you are also learning the skills of communicating through writing.

Hints and tips

- Do write something – anything you write can be improved. Just write something!
- Do not expect to produce a masterpiece – the process is just as important as the end result.
- Do not try to write too much – quality matters, not quantity.
- Do not rely on the computer spell-checker.
- Do not struggle in silence.

- Speak to your academic tutor or fellow students.
- Planning your work is crucial. Spend as much time planning as you do writing.
- Get your skills ready for academic writing using university support
- Ensure you know what you are expected to answer; deconstructing the title is a crucial first step.
- Focus your reading material to make the most of your time.
- Use a method to plan your content for the main body of the essay.
- Organise your material so that the reader understands what you are saying.
- Practice makes you a better writer, so be prepared to rewrite an essay several times before you can hand it in.
- Reading your work aloud can help the flow of your essay.
- For most essays, using evidence to support your argument is the bedrock of academic writing. Writing loaded with personal opinion is weak.
- Use the fewest and simplest words as possible; this will make your writing clearer and easier to understand.
- Use a thesaurus to find alternative words with similar meanings. A useful internet resource is the *Merriam-Webster OnLine Dictionary*, accessed via the following URL: http://www.m-w.com/home.htm.
- Seek feedback on your presentation, including grammar, punctuation and spelling.
- Trust your instincts. You will know whether something looks or sounds wrong.

References

Brookhart, S. (2008) *How to Give Effective Feedback to Students*. Alexandria, VA: Association for Supervision and Curriculum Development.

du Boulay, D. (2000) *What Is an Academic Essay?* www.sussex.ac.uk/langc/ skills/ac-essay.html (accessed 30 Jan. 2013).

Collins (2009) *English Dictionary: Complete & Unabridged* (10th edn). Glasgow: HarperCollins.

Hurley, U. (2012) *Introduction to Academic Writing.* www.hope.ac.uk/doc-man/writing-centre (accessed 30 April 2012).

Juwah, C., Macfarlane-Dick, D. et al. (2004) *Enhancing Student Learning Through Effective Formative Feedback.* www.heacademy.ac.uk/assets/ documents/resources/database/id353_senlef_guide.pdf (accessed 4 July 2012).

King, G. (2000) *Good Grammar.* Glasgow: HarperCollins.

Open University (2003) *What Is Academic Writing?* www3.open.ac.uk/learn-ers-guide/learning-skills/english//sect2/section2summary.htm   (accessed 12 Jan. 2013).

Plain-English-Campaign (2012) www.plainenglish.co.uk/law.html (accessed 30 Jan. 2013).

Trask, R. L. (2000) *The Penguin Dictionary of English Grammar.* London: Penguin.

4

Advancing your writing skills

Carol Lewis-Roylance

This chapter explores the following topics:

- What is different about writing at university?
- Levels of academic writing
- How to think differently and write at the next level
- Descriptive writing
- What is explanation?
- What is argument?
- What is analysis?
- What is evaluation?
- What is synthesis?

Introduction

Writing is the means through which examinations and course-work are assessed, and therefore developing good writing skills is essential to your academic progress. Additionally, writing for publication is a key aspect of professional development, making such skills all the more important. This chapter explores the main features of the six specific styles of writing expected of you at university: description, explanation, argument, analysis, evaluation and synthesis. This chapter clearly identifies the differences between each of these types of writing and guides you through a range of examples and activities to help you understand each of them more fully.

As this chapter is intended for students at all levels of study, you should not be put off by reading terms that may be unfamiliar or new to you as examples and activities are provided to help you understand terms more fully. By the end of this chapter you should be able to:

- recognise the differences between writing at levels 4, 5, 6 and 7
- distinguish between different styles of written text
- apply appropriate writing styles to the theoretical aspect of your course
- understand how cognitive (mental processing) skills can increase your writing potential.

What is different about writing at university?

Students embarking on studies in higher education (HE) face the transition in different ways. Some may be self-assured in their abilities whilst others may feel anxious about this level of study. It is therefore important to understand the different expectations of a student at university. In particular, responsibility for learning lies with the learner. With the increased emphasis on e-learning not all modules are now face to face and learners have limited access to tutors. Other differences include the following:

- Self-management of own workload and time management.
- Development of abilities such as communication and group work skills and applying them to practice.
- Adherence to procedures and guidelines of external governing bodies.
- Understanding individual needs by acknowledging both strengths and challenges.

Studies in HE go beyond simply acquiring knowledge. Showing how you apply theoretical knowledge into practice, using independent thought rather than passive involvement, is also important. Such independent decision making relies on processing information at different levels, from simple to more complex concepts, including:

- Demonstrating and applying newly acquired competencies into practice.
- Critically reflecting on personal and professional issues.
- Understanding and presenting arguments using reason and logic.
- Developing creative thinking to solving problems.
- Consolidating specific academic skills.

Levels of academic writing

A model of learning used in developing suitable curricula objectives at different levels of study is shown in Figure 4.1. These levels closely relate to the learning outcomes in the marking criteria used by your tutors. Therefore you should familiarise yourself with these outcomes at the start of each module. The model shows the hierarchy of learning skills, beginning with *remembering* or gaining knowledge, followed by *understanding* or comprehension of your subject. This is followed by the *application* of your acquired skills into practice, before using the more complex intellectual skills of *analysing, evaluating* and *creating*. It models a learner's intellectual development. For example, a first-year undergraduate would need to acquire knowledge of their subject before comprehension and application are possible. A second-year undergraduate is likely to master knowledge and understanding whilst showing clear relationships with practice in an analytical way. A third-year undergraduate would be expected to

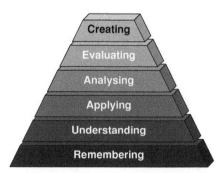

Figure 4.1 Bloom's revised taxonomy of learning (Krathwohl 2002, cited in Atherton 2011)

demonstrate that they can move beyond these levels by attempting to evaluate and create new ideas. Postgraduate students are expected to demonstrate competencies at all levels. Understanding this model is the key to understanding how you are assessed at each stage of your course. Examples of each are shown below.

A first-year student may write the following to show *remembering* **and** *understanding* **of a topic:**
Work stress can affect a person's health. For instance, one in five people experience stress at work and half a million workers had stress related health problems (Directgov 2012).

A second-year student may develop the topic to show how it *applies* **in practice:**
Too much work stress can have a negative impact on a person's health and well-being. According to Directgov (2012), one in five people experience some form of stress at work, with half a million reporting that workplace stress had resulted in illness. This suggests that excessive stress levels at work can result in ill health. For example, . . .

A third-year student may write in a similar style to the above but go on to *analyse, evaluate* **and** *create* **ideas. He or she may also use more linking words (shown in italics) to demonstrate the direction of their argument.**
Too much work stress . . . *etc*. *However*, recent research has shown some stress can be . . . (source), which highlights the complexity of the argument. *This departs* from earlier evidence . . . (source). *In fact*, . . . (source). *Overall*, the evidence points to a revised view which. . . .

Postgraduate writing should demonstrate all six levels of the learning model, including knowledge and understanding, a convincing analytical style, an evaluation and creative thinking. He or she should be able to exploit anomalies in different sources to build counter-arguments, whilst demonstrating insightful understanding of the chosen subject.

How to think differently and write at the next level

Understanding the idea of hierarchical levels of thinking and how these levels apply to you, as a learner, is key to thinking differently and developing your writing ability. Being able to think differently whilst at the same time advancing your writing ability are two skills that develop from a greater self-awareness of your cognitive strengths and weaknesses. One effective way of understanding both skills is to evaluate your own academic performance. Judging your performance objectively and honestly against the marking criteria is key to this process, as is addressing any feedback from your tutors, especially where the intended learning outcomes of the module have not been met. Thinking differently involves recognising shortcomings in key areas of academic performance, especially in writing, as it is often the main method of assessment. For instance, answering your assignment brief and meeting learning outcomes involves several skills:

• Clarifying the assignment brief.
• Sourcing appropriate literature.
• Planning/structuring ideas.
• Developing your main argument.
• Using appropriate academic language.
• Editing and redrafting.

Recognition of any shortcomings you may have in these areas is the first step towards making improvements. Your university library will have a wide variety of books on study skills which provide examples of how to strengthen these general abilities. However, developing specific writing skills moves beyond these general skills, in that writing at university level also requires an understanding of different forms of writing for different purposes. This involves demonstrating your ability to *describe, explain, argue, analyse, evaluate* and *synthesise*, so that you can select the 'best fit' for your intended purpose and assessment requirements. Before examining each of the six writing styles it is important to note that writing for academic purposes, relies on reading a wide variety of published works and selecting relevant literature to support your ideas. In the same way, the following sections draw on both reading and writing examples to better model how to express these styles in your own writing. We are now going to look at these six skills to show how you can become a more confident, expressive and authoritative writer.

Descriptive writing

Descriptive writing is often used when providing a background to a patient's or client's condition or situation. Medical professionals use it when communicating physiological signs and symptoms, whereas a social worker may use it when documenting assessments on individuals or families in crisis. However, a recurring theme on student assignment feedback forms and the reason why marks are lost is that the writing is 'too descriptive'. Often this is because a student has begun by setting the scene or context of the text and not developed it beyond simply telling a story. Sometimes it occurs from placing too much reliance on the source without questioning or developing the main idea in a discursive way, possibly due to insufficient knowledge and understanding of the subject. It also suggests a lack of development in the student's tone, voice and overall style of writing, due in part to the use of informal rather than formal academic language. Yet descriptive writing is an important element in the academic writing process as it supports other writing objectives such as developing an argument, as well as examining issues in critical reflection on practice.

What makes a good descriptive text?

Good descriptive writing has a strong theme using a wide vocabulary which shows the reader a scene or event, whether past, present or future, in rich detail, in order for the reader to sense the scene as if they were there themselves. To accomplish this, writers adopt precise vocabulary to explore the senses, including sight, sound, touch, taste and smell; for instance, using adjectives such as 'anxious' or 'apprehensive' to show feelings in a reflective writing (see Chapter 5).

How does it work?

The building blocks of descriptive writing include the use of the following:

- **specific nouns**, e.g. dictionary (the noun is the book)
- **strong verbs**, e.g. demolish, destroy (improve writing by directing the action of the sentence)
- **adjectives**, e.g. fast, fearful
- **adverbs**, e.g. quickly, boldly
- **sensory words**, e.g. glimpse, radiant, shadowy

as well as simple, compound and complex sentences. These give a richly detailed text that is informative and allows further explanation or argument to be developed.

How is it used?

The description of an endoscopy procedure in Example 1 uses a choice of verbs and adjectives to convey detailed information in a logical sequence.

Example 1

Endoscopy

This involves the passage of a long, flexible bundle of fibre-optic lights. Images are reflected back to the head of the endoscope to provide the operator with a clear picture of the tissues/organs being viewed. It is possible for the operator to obtain samples of tissue for histological examination. A pair of special forceps is passed through the endoscope to the area requiring biopsy. The tissue is then retrieved through the endoscope and sent to the laboratory. Cells for cytological examination can also be obtained via endoscopic examinations.

(Gabriel 2004: 10)

All writers use this type of writing when illustrating events or processes, including health professionals.

Developing a wide subject vocabulary will enhance your descriptions. Example 2 illustrates simple, compound and complex sentences which are the building blocks of descriptive writing.

Example 2

A *simple* sentence: The doctor prescribed analgesics.

A *compound* sentence: The doctor prescribed analgesics, but she failed to sign the prescription.

A *complex* sentence: The doctor prescribed analgesics, while the patient slept.

Putting ideas together in a descriptive way (see italicised words):

The *inexperienced junior* doctor researched the correct dosage and drug compatibility before prescribing the *badly injured* patient with strong analgesia and anti-inflammatory medication.

Describing the main features of something

Example: The National Health Service

Established in 1948 in a beleaguered post-war Britain, still under food rationing restrictions, the National Health Service (NHS) was created to meet the medical needs of the whole population 'from cradle to grave', through national taxation. It brought together three key medical services, hospitals, general practitioners (GPs) and local authorities which had previously operated independently, to form preventative, diagnostic and treatment services under one umbrella. It inherited 480,000 beds from ex-municipal and voluntary hospitals, along with 20,000 GPs previously in private practice. Over 60 years later, the NHS remains the largest publicly funded health service in the world.

To recap

- Use strong verbs, adjectives and specific nouns.
- Utilise different types of sentences, simple, compound and complex.
- Include a wide vocabulary to create rich detail.

Activity 4.1 Descriptive writing

Use the following example as a model and practise writing a simple sentence that conveys one idea, then a compound sentence with two ideas of equal standing. Finally, write a complex sentence with a main idea and a subordinate idea. Once you have achieved this you can insert descriptive words to add specific details.

Simple sentence: Nurses provide patient care.	
Compound sentence: Nurses provide patient care and they carry out prescribed treatments.	
Complex sentence: Nurses provide patient care, despite staff shortages.	

What is explanation?

Another essential prerequisite for clinicians, nurses and other health professionals is effective communication. This often involves providing explanations based on the *purpose, meaning* or *causal nature* of something. For instance, you might be required to explain the purpose of obtaining consent from a patient or client before carrying out any treatment or care. Or you might have to explain the meaning of a diagnosis or condition by interpreting what it signifies in a physiological and/or psychosocial way. An explanation of a causal relationship might be how respiratory problems can result from smoking.

What makes a good explanation?

Good explanations elaborate on a subject whilst using clear and concise language. This clarity will help you to highlight relationships between important points and demystify difficult concepts.

How does it work?

Using purpose, meaning and causation, explanations can explore concepts, processes and procedures as well as relationships. They provide meaningful insights by interpreting knowledge of past processes or events and by showing how they came into being: essentially providing an understanding of something to someone by bridging the gap between knowledge and understanding.

How is it used?

Example 1 offers an explanation of the purpose and value of mentorship in role inculcation of newly qualified nurses. It uses two analogies, the 'grandmother' and 'new robes', to illustrate that it takes time to fully identify with a new professional role.

Example 1

Sometimes, a big part of mentorships and preceptorships is giving the protege/apprentice a chance to be the role, to internalize the role. Just like new grandmothers often protest that they don't 'feel' like grandmothers, graduation does not make a nurse feel like a nurse, and promotion does not make a staff nurse feel like a head nurse. New roles, like new robes, have to be worn awhile before they fit comfortably.

(Flynn and Stack 2006: 9)

Example 2 uses motive and purpose to explain the 'progressive approach' in social work by interpreting the power dynamics between a worker and service user.

Example 2

The role of social work in this approach is to enable those who experience oppression to be able to understand and take more control over their lives. . . . It is not about workers being 'experts' but rather it is about them using their skills to facilitate change. The 'expert' in terms of this approach would be the service user who knows his/her life and capabilities. The worker's skills and knowledge would be in relation to the system and the ability to create the conditions and support for service users to restructure or exert their power.

(Watson and West 2006: 20)

Both examples demonstrate a clear and concise style. They also explore purpose and meaning, using enough detail to reinforce the key points. However, if explanations become too long, overly detailed or wordy they can lose focus and meaning.

Why are some explanations more convincing than others?

Just as your voice expresses your style of speaking, your writing also has a style and tone of its own. Examples 1 and 2 below convey the same message but use different styles. Which do you think will gain your reader's attention more effectively?

Example 1

The NHS was created to provide a comprehensive, free to all, medical service, irrespective of wealth or social status. It was designed to prevent inequalities in health care provision, by focussing on the needs of the sick, rather than the ability to pay through fees or insurances.

Example 2

Inequalities in health care provision before the Second World War, most evident in large towns and cities amongst the poorer classes, especially women and children, prompted the creation of the welfare based health care system, the NHS, which focussed on the needs of the sick, rather than the ability to pay.

Both examples attempt to show how the NHS began, the first using 'purpose' and the second 'causal nature'. In addition, there are differences in their tone, as the second is more authoritative in style and therefore conveys a stronger message. This causal link is demonstrated in Figure 4.2.

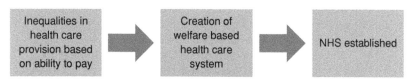

Figure 4.2 An example of a causal link argument

Remember that the desired outcome of a good explanation is for the intended audience to have a greater understanding of the links between X and Y, for example, smoking and cancer.

To recap

- Check what the reader knows or needs to know and prepare relevant information/evidence which builds on existing knowledge.
- Elaborate on key points in sufficient detail from the simple to the complex.
- Clarify by making something clearer or more simplified.
- Summarise by giving a condensed version of the main facts/points.

Activity 4.2 Purpose, meaning and cause

Using the recap notes as a guide, explain the purpose, meaning and cause of the following topics, using a clear writing style.

Patient consent (purpose)
Social exclusion (meaning)
High blood pressure (cause)

What is argument?

Unlike an explanation, which draws on causation, purpose or meaning to interpret a fact or situation, argument utilises logic to support a disputable claim (Toulmin 2001). The reasoning or evidence forms the premise/s (or statements) from which a conclusion can be drawn. Therefore, the reasoning must be sufficiently logical and persuasive for this to happen. Understanding how to develop a persuasive argument in your writing is difficult if you are unable to recognise an argument's structure. Therefore, being able to identify and deconstruct the main features of an argument are important skills.

This section draws on the interrelationship between writing and reading as, for academic purposes, evidence is largely drawn from published literature, which readers are expected to deconstruct to assess any inherent strengths and weaknesses. If your written arguments are without supportive evidence from credible published sources they will be less than convincing. Therefore you need to be able to read and deconstruct arguments before writing your own.

What makes a good argument?

The main purpose of an argument is that it should be credible enough so that it cannot be challenged or contradicted. The premises should be believable and support the conclusion being made. Premises are particular statements of what is known, and in inductive arguments they are *specific statements* that help to support/predict a *general conclusion* or claim being made. Convincing arguments depend on how well we are able to infer, through logical reasoning, that the premises do indeed support the conclusion.

Arguments can also be based on deductive reasoning, opposite to the above, whereby the premises are *general statements* from which *specific conclusions* or claims are drawn. Example 1 shows this type of reasoning. If the conclusion naturally follows from the premise/s it is said to be a valid argument.

Example 1

Premise 1: Nurses provide patient care.

Premise 2: Florence Nightingale was a nurse.

Conclusion: Florence Nightingale provided patient care.

How does it work?

If the strength of an argument is dependent upon both the quality of the conclusion (or claim) and the strength of the premises put forward to support it, then you need to consider both when writing. If the premises are unsound or the conclusion is flawed, then your argument is weakened and can be challenged. To avoid this problem in your own writing you will need to make sure your arguments are based on sound premises, which draw on reliable evidence, because if your premises are true then your conclusion cannot be false (as shown in the 'Florence Nightingale' example above). The lesson here is to avoid making an argument that could be challenged by opposing claims. You can do this by either strengthening your premises or, in some instances where your evidence is less robust, weakening your own conclusion to fit it. For instance, if the figure in Example 2 was 50 per cent, the argument would be significantly weaker: hence the conclusion could be challenged.

Example 2

Premise 1: If health care professionals wish to advance their careers they should undertake continuous professional development.

Premise 2: 95 per cent of health care professionals want to advance their careers.

Conclusion: Therefore, most health care professionals should undertake continuous professional development.

How is it used?

There are many types of arguments, using different forms of reasoning: for instance, analogy, sign, cause, example, testimony and narrative (Walton 1996). As a writer, it is important that you consider what type of reasoning you intend to draw upon to support your argument. This will depend on the evidence, which should be high quality, factual or theoretical evidence. Also, you should source your evidence using academic databases, rather than Google, as internet sources cannot always be verified. If you are unsure how to find relevant sources, seek support from your university's library service.

Structure

An argument should include three basic elements:

- a conclusion or claim
- evidence
- reasoning

It is considered good practice to include two further elements:

- a warrant, which is the persuasive logic that connects the evidence to the claim
- alternative viewpoints or counter-claims

When asked to discuss a subject or issue as part of a written assessment, you are expected to present your ideas in the form of a balanced argument, which should address alternative viewpoints. Essentially, your argument should attempt to bring about a change in your reader's understanding on a particular issue (Rosenwasser and Stephen 2009).

Planning and writing up your argument

1 Consider your viewpoint (or claim) regarding your chosen subject, and whether you have sufficient evidence to support it.
2 Avoid settling for a simple viewpoint, for instance: 'The NHS is the greatest health care provider in the world.' Instead, consider a more specific viewpoint such as 'The NHS is a significant health care provider, but its greatest impact has been in medical science, especially organ transplantation.'
3 Acknowledge alternative viewpoints (counter-arguments/claims) and be prepared to explore these by evaluating the supportive reasoning and evidence objectively.
4 Show how your own viewpoint has more merit.
5 Now gather the evidence that best supports the logical chain of reasoning (warrant) that connects the evidence to your claim.
6 You are now ready to write up your argument.
7 Start with:
    (a) An explanatory introduction, including a thesis statement that contains your viewpoint.
    (b) Present both sides of the subject by discussing the counter-argument in depth.

(c) Note the strengths and weaknesses of the counter-argument and highlight the strongest point.

(d) Present your own viewpoint showing it has more merit.

(e) Back up your own viewpoint with relevant factual and theoretical evidence.

(f) Use effective paraphrasing rather than direct quotations as it helps you to develop your own authoritative voice/style.

8 Restate your viewpoint in your summary.

Points to consider in your written arguments

- Any assertions (statements or claims) you make must be self-evident, otherwise they will need supporting, for example: 'The NHS is facing its *worst economic crisis* since it was established.'
- Avoid rash generalisations, for example: 'MRSA is *rife* in hospitals.'
- Only use persuasive words when the evidence justifies their use, for example: '*Clearly*, social workers are under pressure with unmanageable workloads.'
- Avoid leaving your reader drawing his or her own conclusions. Instead, establish your claim first, then build your premises/ reasons to support it.

Putting an argument together

Example

Inequalities in health care provision, spanning many decades, have undermined the legitimacy of NHS principles, established in 1948. By 1980, the fundamental principle of equality of health care in the NHS was being questioned by the Black Report. This report highlighted the differences between social classes in their use of health services and found stark inequalities in infant mortality and life expectancy rates, arguing that poorer people were more at risk from premature death. Its findings were endorsed by two later reports in 1987 and 1998; showing little had changed in almost 20 years. In addition, as advances in both technology and pharmacology resulted in variations in the quality of care and treatment in England and Wales, the government attempted to combat this 'postcode lottery'. As a consequence, the National Institute for Health and Clinical Excellence (NICE) was established in 1999, to provide evidence-based guidelines to commissioners of health services, in both areas. This shows that the principles, of accessible health care for all, continue to challenge successive governments.

Use of analogy, signs and causes to substantiate an argument

Analogy
When building your argument using an analogy, consider whether the similarities between the two cases are stronger than the differences. If they are, then the analogy is a good one and, most importantly, will provide support for the conclusion.

Example

Drinking above the recommended UK limits for alcohol consumption and the use of cannabis causes teenagers to become more sexually active and get into arguments and fights (Newbury-Birch et al. 2000). First-year medical students indulging in excessive alcohol and cannabis also become more sexually involved and experience conflict situations. Teenagers also miss schooling due to excessive drinking and drug taking. Therefore, medical students who drink excessively and take illicit drugs are at risk of missing periods of study.

Sign
Sign can be used in arguments when the evidence is characteristic of a wider principle.

Example

The patient's bloods contained low levels of haemoglobin and reduced red blood cells. These results are an indicator of anaemia. Therefore the patient is likely to have anaemia.

When using sign as an argument, consider whether there is an alternative explanation.

Cause
Cause can be used to show that a particular event is the result of, or effected by, X.

Example

The widespread use of antibiotics has given rise to resistant bacteria and consequently, to an increase in hospital acquired infections.

When using cause, consider if X really caused Y and whether other causes may explain the effect.

To recap

When writing arguments:

- Use a clearly specified line of persuasive reasoning.
- Use quality factual or theoretical evidence in your reasoning.
- Ensure your premises strongly support your conclusion.

Activity 4.3 Concluding statement

Read the following concluding statement and choose one reason which provides the most compelling case.

Junior doctors' long working hours should be reduced because:

1 There is a strong correlation between working long hours and clinical negligence.
2 Working long hours is dangerous to health.
3 Junior doctors are overworked.

What is analysis?

Analysis is the art of taking something apart to examine its constituent parts, to better understand it. It involves a questioning approach such as a detective would use in trying to solve a criminal case. We all analyse things in our everyday lives. This is especially true of young children; for example, if a toddler is given a new toy he or she will invariably attempt to take it apart to examine how it works. In the field of academia, analytical thinking allows us to judge a work's significance and assess whether the arguments presented add to existing theories or present new ones. As discussed in the previous section on arguments, this is likely to involve breaking down a body of text to assess its claim and premises or supportive reasoning to see if it is a valid argument, or whether you are able to make a counter-argument. This involves assessing the strengths and weaknesses of each premise and the claim itself. It also means considering what is true and not accepting facts or opinions at face value. This brings us back to the analogy of the detective who, in trying to discover the truth, must identify false arguments by recognising how and why they have occurred.

What makes a good analysis?

Critical thinking and evaluation skills are employed in analysis, especially when exploring the positive and negative aspects of something. When it comes to analysing other people's written arguments, a questioning approach is necessary to determine the relevancy and adequacy of each premise, to determine possible fallacies (unsound reasoning) and alternative explanations, or indeed any assumptions, bias or ambiguity. When writing your own analysis, it is good to remember the critical stance of your audience in this way.

Example

To clarify a point: 'What exactly does this mean?'

To question assumptions: 'How can the assumption be verified?'

To query the rationale: 'What evidence is there to support it?'

To question viewpoints: 'What are their strengths and weaknesses?'

To explore the consequences: 'What are the implications?'

How do analysis and argument differ from one another? As we discovered in the previous section, an argument is designed to bring about a change in the reader's understanding on a particular issue, whereas analysis is more about the writer setting out his or her own understanding on a subject (Rosenwasser and Stephen 2009).

How does it work?

Investigative journalists draw on analytical skills to assess the facts of any given subject before exploiting any inconsistencies in the claims. They use questions such as who, what, why, when or how to understand and break down arguments, to expose possible weaknesses or fallacies. They also identify controversial issues that may lead to a counter-argument. They then set about exploiting what they have discovered in their own analysis on the subject. Adopting this approach will help you to engage at a deeper level of thinking and, most importantly, enhance your own analytical writing.

Example

A recent media story from the online newspaper *The Observer* (Doward 2012), 'Rat population will rocket if pest poisons are restricted, experts fear', discusses the Health and Safety Executive's plans to restrict the application of certain rat poisons within the UK, as they believe these poisons are now overused and consequently killing other types of wildlife such as birds.

How would you begin to question this argument to expose possible weaknesses in order to help you identify an alternative viewpoint? The journalist has already suggested one critical angle in the title of the article: what effect this policy will have on the rat population. Can you think of any more? You could, for example, ask the following questions:

- What effect will the policy have in general?
- How will it impact on people's health?
- Will it affect property prices in urban areas?
- Is there an alternative deterrent to manage the rat population which does not harm birds?
- Should the role of rat catchers be reinstated?

Note that some of these questions are very specific and could lead to a variety of interesting counter-arguments.

How is it used?

For health professionals in particular, analysis is important in understanding how theory impacts on practice and vice versa. For example, you would not take the patient's own diagnosis of their medical condition at face value and treat accordingly. Instead, you would use scientific tests and rigorously analyse results to show causation and seek the most effective evidence-based treatment. This method, based on the epidemiologist Bradford Hill's criterion for analysing cause and effect (Hofler 2005), enables health professionals to identify and categorise problems, to make comparisons and find solutions.

Demonstrating analysis in your own writing

Having explored some of the key elements in analytical writing, here are the main points to remember:

1 Suspend judgement on your chosen issue as your role as a writer is to remain objective.
2 Be a detective and look at the general picture first before examining specific aspects.

3 Break it down into its constituent parts: can you detect any bias or ambiguity?
4 Question how the parts are related.
5 Do not forget to show your reader how it all fits back together again.
6 Identify and discuss any significant patterns or implications.
7 Be clear about any inferences you are drawing from the evidence.

Writing using an analytical style

Before the advent of the National Health Service, compared to voluntary hospitals, the publically funded poor law hospitals had far fewer doctors and nurses, limited specialist facilities, higher patient: doctor ratios and longer bed occupancy rates. Throughout the 1920s, medics were influential in developing poor law hospital services on the voluntary hospital model. This included new theatres to treat more acute surgical cases, as well as diagnostic facilities including bacteriology, pathology and radiography, which together shortened the average length of stay of patients in hospital. This increased professionalisation of the service meant, by the 1930s, poor law hospitals were more on a par with voluntary hospitals. Yet, the stigma of association with destitution remained a strong deterrent for the working class population, long after these hospitals were nationalised in 1948.

(Lewis-Roylance 2005)

The passage above uses many of the key elements of analytical writing. It *breaks down* the subject of pre-NHS hospitals into two types: voluntary and poor law hospitals. It *examines the differences* between them and then how they *relate to one another*. It also points out the *significance* of medics in the development of poor law hospitals before suggesting the similar *patterns* that developed over time. Notably, it *infers* the lack of support from the working-class population because of the stigma of destitution.

Figure 4.3 has been included to help you visualise the sequence of the previous example. Now put your detective hat on and consider what questions you would ask in order to expose a possible counter-argument.

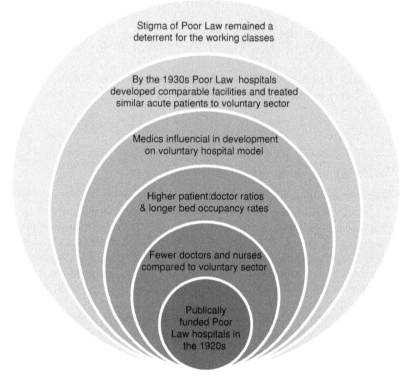

Figure 4.3 Sequence of reasoning

Adopting a questioning approach will help you to identify the strengths and weaknesses of the rationale and viewpoint and identify your counter-argument, for example:

1 What type of evidence is there to support the claim? There may be statistical evidence from the hospitals on the numbers of working-class admissions.
2 Was the stigma widespread throughout the country or patchy? Look for trends in geographical data.
3 How much influence did medics actually have at that time? Question the role of the Poor Law guardians, as they were responsible for managing these services.

Breaking down arguments and counter-arguments is a skill best developed by critical reading. Question how credible an author's argument is by examining each premise and claim, checking each is relevant, adequate and without bias. Incorporate these skills to your own writing by ensuring you address any possible counter-argument, as this will add balance and strength to your own argument. Demonstrating analysis in this way requires a degree of clarity in making valid and logical points, as without this the reader is unable to follow your argument. To this end, signposting of evidence using linking words or phrases is important. The following words are good examples of things to look for in writing to indicate what is a premise and what is a concluding statement, so use them in your own work as they will help your reader to focus on your points and follow your intended direction.

Premises: 'because', 'as', 'since', 'assuming that' or 'may be inferred'.

Conclusions: 'therefore', 'consequently' or 'suggests'.

To recap

- Break down a text to assess the claim.
- Analyse the validity and logic of the reasoning.
- Use a questioning approach to assess the strengths and weaknesses.
- Question possible alternative claims.
- Structure arguments using clear signposting, selection and sequencing of evidence.

Activity 4.4 Flaws

A questioning approach will help you find flaws (or fallacies) and challenge claims. For example, can you detect a flaw in the following argument?

Some patients are concerned about the level of MRSA in hospitals. Therefore, all patients are neurotic.

Question whether the reasoning is:

- based on factual or theoretical evidence
- logical and attempts to persuade
- relevant and adequate enough to support the claim.

Did you notice that the premise does not provide adequate reasoning for the conclusion 'all patients are neurotic' to be accepted? Therefore the argument is 'flawed'.

What is evaluation?

Evaluation is the result of judging the value or merit of an argument or theory through supportive reasoning. Also comparing one thing with another, for example, to determine how well a given set of data from the present compares with similar data from the past. Evaluation is central to understanding health and social care interventions, as without it how would we know whether an intervention was successful?

What makes a good evaluation?

Like analysis, evaluation requires a questioning approach to prove the merits of an argument or process against a criterion or framework. Useful questions include the following:

- How well did it work?
- How do we know?
- What needs to change?
- What will I do differently?

These are particularly relevant in reflective writing where behaviours and attitudes are evaluated against expected professional norms to ultimately improve future practice.

It is also good practice to evaluate the strength of your writing as you progress through your studies by paying particular attention to its tone and style. For instance, there are clear differences in style between the two examples below.

Example 1

We have all forgotten to gel our hands on entering a hospital ward. You see health care staff forgetting to do this all the time. Yet hand hygiene saves lives.

This example is personal and draws on the author's own subjective observations.

Example 2

Research has shown that not all health care staffs comply with hand hygiene procedures on entry to hospital wards (source). Yet hand hygiene almost certainly helps to save lives (source).

This example is more objective in style and draws on supportive evidence.

The categorical position in example one is assertive and leaves little room for argument, whereas example two concludes with a non-categorical (less assertive) standpoint that uses evidence to persuade the reader, whilst demonstrating a possible alternative viewpoint. Consider these stylistic differences when writing your own evaluative accounts.

How does it work?

In the case of a patient receiving physiotherapy, we may ask how well a specific exercise regime worked, to what degree, and whether there were any barriers to carrying out the exercises. Feedback from questions would help the physiotherapist assess the efficacy of the intervention and identify necessary changes, such as adopting more holistic and effective alternative exercises for a particular patient's ability level, lifestyle and circumstances. In this way evaluative questions establish whether processes do or do not work, and why. For example, evaluation of hospital statistics in 'mortality', 'hospital acquired infections' and 'reported safety incidents' provide evidence for future decision making (see Activity 4.5).

How is it used?

Literature reviews are good academic examples of how evaluation works, as the purpose is to compare evidence, methodologies and findings from different sources, to identify the similarities and differences in their arguments. This enables you to find gaps in existing knowledge and show how this understanding relates to your own research. Students are often asked to demonstrate their evaluation skills by writing literature reviews as part of assessments, particularly dissertation studies.

Evaluations also involve clinical evidence, for example: Imagine you are a member of NICE's Centre for Health Technology Evaluation, producing recommendations on the usefulness of a new medicine. To do this, you are required to evaluate the clinical and economic evidence for and against the medicine. Read the list below and consider the types of questions you need to ask to accomplish this?

1 Does it work?
2 Is it cost effective?
3 Who will benefit?
4 Is it safe?
5 What are the alternatives?

Most people would correctly identify the first two questions. The first would help to assess the clinical evidence by carrying out an evaluation of the effects of the medicine on a target group. The second would help to assess the economic evidence by conducting a cost-benefit analysis. Look at the 'published appraisals' on the following link to see how NICE evaluates new medicines/treatments: www.nice.org.uk/guidance/index.jsp?status=3&d-16544-p=6&action=byType&type=6

Once you have conducted a clinical evaluation or literature review you are ready to write it up.

The nuts and bolts of writing in an evaluative style

- Avoid being subjective and judgemental.
- Set the issue you are evaluating into context.
- Be clear what criteria you are using and review them.
- Avoid unnecessary details and stay on point.
- Use comparisons and contrasts to show balance.
- Provide evidence to back up your opinions.
- Show your reader that you are weighing up the pros and cons objectively.
- Step down off the fence and argue your position/opinion.

Example

In order to evaluate X's argument on the efficacy of diet pills, as a means of weight loss, it is important to assess the reasoning. *The author fails to* attest that the ingredients have clinically proven benefits in weight loss, as there is a clear difference between a clinically approved ingredient and a mixed compound within a pill (Alkinson 2012). *Neither does X address* the health risks, which research has shown can manifest as health-compromising behaviours such as substance abuse (Neumark-Sztainer et al.1998). *For these reasons, in my opinion*, the effects of diet pills have been overstated.

Useful phrases in evaluative writing:

- In order to assess X's argument we need to . . .
- X offers no evidence for . . .
- What X fails to consider is . . . .
- Arguably, X is opposite to Y
- X seems to attach too much significance to . . .
- X makes many valid points
- There is clearly a difference between . . .
- The problem with X's theory is . . . as it does not address . . .
- In general I agree with . . . although I think that . . .

To recap

Evaluation:

- involves judging the value or merit of something
- uses a questioning approach
- influences decision making
- can determine the success or failure of health care interventions.

Activity 4.5 Evaluating data

Evaluate the evidence in the sample table below, bearing in mind that hospitals below 100 had fewer deaths, whereas hospitals above this figure had more deaths than expected. What does it suggest?

Mortality rates (number of hospital deaths in one year)			
Hospital A	Hospital B	Hospital C	Hospitals D
91	95	115	112

Evaluating data can help define the scope of a problem and show where the problem lies and the types of decisions needed to rectify causes, such as measuring quality of care in hospitals. Now write a brief report on your findings, using evaluative type phrases to direct your reader to your position.

What is synthesis?

Synthesising allows us to blend old and new ideas together to form fresh insights that can alter our perceptions. In practitioner terms, think about how your professional knowledge adapts through new research-based evidence to continuously improve practice.

What makes good synthesis?

Unlike analysis, which examines one particular idea in detail, synthesis involves discussing several viewpoints, showing your understanding of them, to the point where you are able to offer a fresh perspective on the subject and make new connections, for example, between practice and theory. This process is the eureka moment, when we fully comprehend an idea for the first time and understand its application. This often results in original and creative solutions to problems.

How does it work?

Synthesis is about understanding ideas at a deeper level, as new connections between ideas become clearer. Showing these connections in your writing demonstrates an awareness of new possibilities, making creative thinking more likely. It also demonstrates that you have researched widely, using factual and theoretical sources to help you make credible arguments.

How is it used?

We use synthesis every day when we make informed decisions about our lives. For instance, the effect of not having enough eggs to make a favourite cake recipe may prevent us from cooking. However, we might have the creative insight to halve the ingredients to make a smaller mix. This solution aims to maximise the advantages of available ingredients whilst reducing the disadvantages of not baking our favourite cake.

Another example is that of Florence Nightingale. She used various sources of evidence gathered from her travels across Europe that enabled her to synthesise information on nursing care. She went on to develop radically different ideas from her contemporaries on how to professionalise care in workhouse institutions in England, from able-bodied paupers to trained nurses.

In academic terms, systematic reviews of literature are good examples of synthesis in action because they draw evidence from different studies such as randomised control trials. When compared to a single study, multiple studies reduce the level of bias, making results more reliable. This is synthesising at its best as it often leads to new insights. When writing, you should try to synthesise using this type of high quality source as it is evidence based and therefore more appropriate in the field of health care.

How to write using synthesis

1 Choose several texts and summarise each of the main points.
2 Try to assess where the ideas overlap with one another.
3 Assess any similarities and differences.
4 Generalise these ideas in a logical way around a theme.
5 Show you are thinking and making connections about a theme at a deeper level.
6 Support your own argument with evidence.
7 Summarise your main point.

Writing using synthesis

The following passage uses four such publications, synthesised together, to show the value of evidence-based research.

To support the decision-making process on patient care, evidence-based practice needs to be systematic, both in the quality of data and its detailed examination (Stuart 2001). In this way, evidence-based practice is key to justifying health care expenditures (Chapman et al. 2007). However, barriers to best practice, through uninformed clinicians, can hinder progress (Spring 2008), jeopardising health outcomes for patients, despite easily accessible systematic reviews in reliable repositories such as the Cochrane database (Mullen et al. 2008). This suggests that clinicians could make more use of evidence-based research to inform their decision making.

To recap

Synthesis involves:

• independent thinking and fresh perspectives
• creative solutions to problems using new insights.

Activity 4.6 Synthesis

Using the example above, find several articles in your specialism on one area of research. Assess their main arguments/claims. What insights do they suggest in your specialist field? Follow points 1-7 above to write your own synthesis.

Conclusion

Advancing specific writing skills is a developmental process, the success of which depends on how much attention you give to it, such as reading tutor feedback and understanding the marking criteria. The following specific writing skills – description, explanation, argument, analysis, evaluation and synthesis – each have a part to play in developing your writing style, as your academic progress is measured on how well you demonstrate them. In particular, reading credible published works will enhance greater awareness of good writing techniques. Moreover, a questioning approach is important, especially in identifying flawed arguments, as this will strengthen your own critical analysis and evaluation skills. Essentially, if you engage with tasks by looking for meaning and not taking a superficial approach to learning, you will reap positive results in your writing. Finally, if this chapter has stimulated your interest in advancing specific writing skills, the web resources at the end of the chapter provide further models of good practice.

Hints and tips

- Descriptions should be rich and detailed.
- Explore cause, meaning or purpose in explanations.
- Ensure arguments are based on persuasive reasoning.
- Question the relevancy/adequacy of premises to identify unsound reasoning.
- Use a criterion or framework when assessing the merits of interventions.
- Develop new insights to find creative solutions to problems.

Web resources

Produced by Manchester University, this resource illustrates a diverse range of phrases, for use in introductions, discussions and conclusions: www. phrasebank.manchester.ac.uk/introductions.htm

Designed to model writing skills, Plymouth University has produced WrAssE, an e-resource on writing assignments, searchable by subject with examples of essays, plus lecturer comments: www.learningdevelopment. plymouth.ac.uk/wrasse/

LearnHigher, Centre for Excellence in Teaching and Learning, has compiled a repository of resources for students which include academic writing and critical thinking skills: www.learnhigher.ac.uk/students.htm

This comprehensive audio resource from Sheffield University is a study skills resource for dyslexic students, but has a wider application useful to all HE students interested in the building blocks of writing sentences and para-graphs, as well as structuring and developing arguments: dyslexstudyskills. group.shef.ac.uk/

References

Atherton, J. S. (2011) *Learning and Teaching: Bloom's Taxonomy*. www. learningandteaching.info/learning/bloomtax.htm.

Atkinson, L. (2010) Do slimming pills ever work? The very unappetising truths about their impact on your health, *Daily Mail*, 19 October. www. dailymail.co.uk/health/article-1321691/Do-slimming-pills-EVER-work-The-unappetising-truths-impact-health.html (accessed 24 Nov. 2012).

Chapman, G., Sellaeg, K., Levy-Milne, R. and Barr, S. (2007) Towards increased capacity for evidence-based practice among health professionals, *Qualitative Health Research*, 17: 902–907.

Directgov (2012) *Employment: Workplace Stress*. www.direct.gov.uk/en/ Employment/HealthAndSafetyAtWork/DG_10026604.

Doward, J. (2012) Rat population will rocket if pest poisons are restricted, experts fear. *The Observer Online*. www.guardian.co.uk/environment/2012/ nov/18/rat-population-pest-poisons-restricted#start-of-comments (accessed 18 Nov. 2012).

Flynn, J. and Stack, M. (2006) *The Role of the Preceptor: A Guide for Nurse Educators, Clinicians and Managers*. Retrieved from EBSCO.

Gabriel, J. (2004) *The Biology of Cancer*. Retrieved from EBSCO.

Höfler, M. (2005) The Bradford Hill considerations on causation: a coun-terfactual perspective, *Emerging Themes in Epidemiology*, 2(11). www.ete-online.com/content/2/1/11.

Krathwohl, D. (2002) A revision of Bloom's taxonomy: an overview, *Theory and Practice*, 41(4): 212–218. www.jstor.org/stable/1477405.

Lewis-Roylance, C. (2005) General hospital provision in Liverpool in the voluntary and publically funded sectors c. 1918–1938: a comparative study. Unpublished doctoral thesis. Edge Hill University College, Lancaster University.

Mullen, E., Bledsoe, S. and Bellamy, J. (2008) Implementing evidence-based social work practice, *Research on Social Work*, 18: 325–338.

National Institute for Clinical Excellence (NICE, 2012) *Published Appraisals.* www.nice.org.uk/guidance/index.jsp?status=3&d-16544-p=6&action=byType&type=6.

Neumark-Sztainer, D., Story, M., Dixon, L. and Murray, D. (1998) Adolescents engaging in unhealthy weight control behaviors: are they at risk of other health-compromising behaviors, *American Journal of Public Health*, 88(6): 952–955. http://ajph.aphapublications.org/doi/pdf/10.2105/AJPH.88.6.952.

Newbury-Birch, D., White, M. and Kamali, F. (2000) Factors influencing alcohol and illicit drug use amongst medical students, *Drug and Alcohol Dependence*, 59(2): 125–130.

Rogers, S. (2009). Datablog: drop-out rates for every university. *The Guardian.* www.guardian.co.uk/news/datablog/2009/jun/05/accesstouniversity-higher-education (accessed 5 June 2009).

Rosenwasser, D. and Stephen, J. (eds) (2009) *Writing analytically* (5th edn). Boston, MA: Thomson/Wadsworth.

Royal College of Nursing (2008) *Nursing our Future.* www.rcn.org.uk_data/assets/pdf-file0006/281742/003309.pdf.

Spring, B. (2008) Health decision making, *Medical Decision Making*, 28: 866–874.

Stuart, G. (2001) Evidence-based psychiatric nursing practice, *Journal of the American Psychiatric Nurses Association*, 7: 103–114.

Toulmin, S. (2001) *Return to Reason.* Cambridge, MA: Harvard University Press.

Walton, D. (1996) *Argumentation: Schemes for Presumptive Reasoning.* New York: Routledge.

Waters, D. (2008) Nursing student attrition is costing the taxpayers 99 million pounds a year, *Nursing Standard*, 22(31): 12–15. http://nursingstandard.rcnpublishing.co.uk/shared/media/pdfs/v22n31p1215.pdf.

Watson, D. and West, J. (2006) *Social Work Process and Practice: Approaches, Knowledge and Skills.* Retrieved from EBSCO.

5

What is reflective writing?

Jane Quigley

This chapter explores the following topics:

- What is reflective writing?
- Why reflect?
- Types of reflection
- Reflective models
- How to use a reflective model
- How to write reflectively
- Critical reflective writing
- How to structure a reflective essay

Introduction

This chapter begins by describing the process of reflection and explains its importance to you as a student in health and social care. By understanding reflection, you will then be able to apply this process to your practice and academic studies, gaining more knowledge and insight from them, and therefore enhancing your learning. There are many reflective models that can be drawn on to assist you in this process. In this chapter we use two popular reflective models to provide you with clear examples of how to reflect both professionally (practice) and also academically (theory). Suggestions on using a model to record your own thoughts and feelings and then reflect on a recent event are provided. Practical tips on how to write reflectively, how to structure a reflective essay and how to achieve critical reflective writing are included. Reflection is a progressive skill that can be developed throughout your programme in health and social care. The chapter therefore also provides useful information about the development of reflection through to higher levels of study, such as level 6 and masters level (see also Chapter 4). As reflection is an important part of health and social care, this chapter helps you to develop the practical skills of reflection and, further, to demonstrate this skill in your academic endeavours.

What is reflection?

Reflection is the examination of personal thoughts and actions. For health and social care students, this usually means focusing on how you interact with your colleagues and clients/patients to obtain a clearer picture of your own behaviour and reactions to situations. Reflection can make you more aware of your practice and help you to feel more confident in yourself generally and in your professional role. It can help you to make the best use of the knowledge available and successfully challenge and develop existing professional practice. Reflection will enable you to examine your practice which will maximise opportunities for learning and improve your professional judgement by helping you to learn from practice and enhance your understanding and development.

Reflection is a method of learning (Dewey 1997) by linking together new and old experiences. You will learn by 'doing' and become aware that any action has a consequence. The reflective process enables you to question your actions and to make sense of them. This is similar to Kolb's (1985) experiential learning theory which suggests that learners go through a four-stage cycle which begins, as with other theories, with the experience followed by reflection leading to concepts and then future actions.

Reflection is especially useful to those working in areas where critical situations occur often and where there is little time to prepare your response, such as in accident and emergency departments. Following a critical incident, reflection provides you with an opportunity to use a structured process to 'go over' the event, your responses and interactions. This enables you to make sense of the situation and to identify how your strengths had a positive impact on the situation. Conversely, reflection will help you identify personal and professional approaches that would benefit from development. Reflection is an active process that can be supported through the use of a model (sometime referred to as a framework). Some reflective models will be explored later in this chapter.

For you as a student, reflection requires your honesty, time, thought and effort to accurately recall events and experiences as you see them. From this you will develop the ability to examine your personal thoughts and actions with a beneficial effect on your professional practice, beliefs and values.

Why reflect?

We take part in reflection for a number of reasons. It is necessary for you to constantly reflect on practice in order to learn from experiences. It is also in your professional interest to think about how you interact with patients and colleagues as it may illuminate existing personal beliefs, bias and assumptions that impact on your behaviour. Jasper (2003) suggests that reflection is a process that helps us develop strategies for survival throughout our life:

> An inability to build life skills as a result of learning from our experiences puts us at risk. For instance, think of the care and attention that small children need to keep them safe when outside, or the problems that people who suffer from dementia have as a result of 'forgetting' the fundamental lessons of safety in daily life.
>
> (Jasper 2003: 4)

Tips for why reflection is important

- To identify learning needs and opportunities for learning.
- To explore alternative ways of solving problems.
- For personal and professional development.
- To be aware of the consequence of our actions.
- To create opportunities to improve professional competence.
- To gain knowledge from observations.
- To help us make decisions or resolve uncertainty.
- To empower or emancipate ourselves as individuals.
- To develop a new attitude/way of thinking.

(Adapted from Jasper 2003)

Types of reflection

There are two basic forms of reflection: reflection-on-*action* and reflection-in-*action* (Schön 1987). The word *action* is vital. Understanding the differences between these forms of reflection is important.

Reflection-on-action

The most common form of reflection is reflection-on-action. This involves mentally revisiting past events to gain insight and understanding of your personal behaviours. Making such observations would create opportunities to improve your professional competence. For example: 'I could have communicated more effectively by explaining the process of discharge from the ward' or 'I need to improve the detail in which I record events in the clinical records.'

Reflection-in-action

Reflection-in-action is a skill that all health and social care students should strive to achieve and become increasingly proficient at throughout their professional careers. To develop this skill you need to examine your own behaviours and the behaviours of others during an event or interaction (Schön 1995). The following skills are involved:

• Being a participant observer in situations that offer learning opportunities.
• Attending to what you see and feel in your current situation, focusing on your responses and making connections with previous experiences.
• Being 'in the experience' and, at the same time, adopting a 'witness' stance as if you were outside it.

For example, you may be attending a patient in their home to provide care but notice empty whisky bottles on the floor. Using the reflection-in-action approach, you would deal with the immediate care need but simultaneously be mentally preparing to escalate your concern in relation to what the empty bottles may indicate. This approach to reflection-in-action enables you to take a considered approach to managing the situation in a sensitive and meaningful manner. This will lead you to consider carefully the consequences of any potential action you might choose. Reflection-in-action is a skill that is developed with practice. Some helpful tips on developing your skills of reflection will be provided throughout the chapter.

Reflective models

As a reflective practitioner you will need to be able to critically reflect on what you know both academically (theory) and professionally (practice). There are many models you can use to assist in the process of reflection. You may have been introduced to popular reflective models including Johns (2000) and Gibbs (1988). During your studies in health and social care you will be expected to write reflectively about your practice in your academic work. Each of these models is outlined in the boxes below. Later in this chapter we provide an example of how Johns's model can facilitate how you reflect on your practice and how Gibbs's model can be used to write reflectively.

There are various models and they will be useful for different situations. They can be used in practice to reflect on your learning or as a reflective framework for academic writing. Find the one that works for the situation in which you find yourself reflecting. The benefit of reflective practice is that it increases confidence and allows students to become more proactive as professional practitioners. It improves the quality of care given and closes the gap between theory and practice, providing a deeper understanding of our approach to nursing and leading to greater effectiveness as a nurse (Somerville and Keeling 2004). It does not matter which framework you choose or if you decide to adapt and take elements from a number of the frameworks depending on the situation you are reflecting on.

Johns's (2000) model of reflection

- Describing an experience significant to the learner.
- Identifying personal issues arising from the experience.
- Pinpointing personal intentions.
- Empathising with others in the experience.
- Recognising one's own values and beliefs.

- Linking this experience with previous experiences.
- Creating new options for future behaviour.
- Looking at ways to improve working with patients, families and staff in order to meet patients' needs.

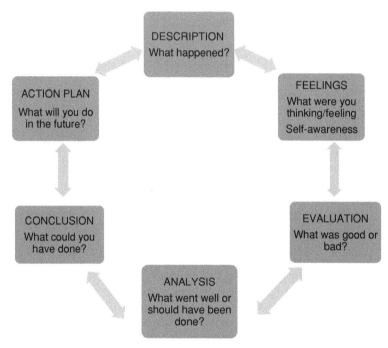

Figure 5.1 Gibbs's (1988) model of reflection

How to use a reflective model

Johns's (2000) model for structured reflection can be used to analyse critical incidents in practice or reflect on experiences. This model advocates looking *inwards* upon the situation and focusing on your thoughts and feelings, whilst also looking *outside* of the situation. This enables you to consider very carefully what you are trying to achieve and why you acted in the way that you did, including how others were affected. Johns also suggests you consider other factors such as the potential anxiety of the situation.

Activity 5.1 Structured reflection

Use this model to record your thoughts and feelings about a recent event.

Areas to cover	Reflection
Description Write a description of the experience thinking specifically about what the key issues are that you need to reflect upon?	
Identify Reflect on any personal issues arising. **Pinpoint** Personal intentions.	
Empathise Consider and reflect on others involved in the experience.	
Reflect and recognise your values and beliefs What were you trying to achieve? Why did you act as you did? What were the consequences of your actions (patient, family, yourself, colleagues)? How did you feel about this experience when it was happening?	
Influencing factors What internal factors influenced your decisions and actions? What external factors influenced your decision and actions? What knowledge influenced your decision making and actions?	
Link with previous experience and alternative strategies Could you have dealt better with the situation? What other choices did you have? What would be the consequences of these other choices?	

Create and look at learning How can you make sense of this experience in light of past experience and future practice? How do you *now* feel about this experience? Have you taken effective action to support yourself and others as a result of this experience? How has this experience changed the way you practice?	

(Adapted from Johns 2000)

How to write reflectively

Reflective writing in health and social care is a way of evaluating and improving practice. Reflective writing is the physical written result of the reflection process. According to Moon (2004) there are factors that could shape your reflection into reflective writing. These might include the reason why you are writing reflectively: for example, personal reasons such as in a diary or as part of an academic assignment. It may depend on whether others are going to see what you have written and who they are, friends or colleagues, a tutor who will mark it or a tutor who will not mark it. Reflection is also affected by your emotional state at the time of writing, and emotional reaction to what you are writing about: for example, a critical incident in practice or alternatively something you did well. Much of what you write will depend on who may see it.

You can develop and demonstrate your knowledge and skills by using a reflective approach to your writing. Your reflection on your personal and professional experiences may lead you to develop and enhance your self-awareness, understanding and knowledge of the many events you will encounter. It may also help you in establishing the link between theory and practice.

It is acceptable to use the first person 'I' in reflective writing, but remember reflective writing is not a descriptive exercise. A simple description of an event does not provide the opportunity to question your own involvement, neither does it create opportunities for you to learn from it. Reflection will, for example, involve you questioning yourself and others. You will find adopting a reflective approach to be a rewarding experience as it illuminates the how and why of your values and beliefs. It also provides the opportunity to change or adapt them as required. Thus, it should be a meaningful process.

Your reflective writing should move from superficial descriptive writing on to a more questioning and thoughtful analysis. Reflection can be seen as the bridge that connects past and present experiences.

Table 5.1 Example of reflective writing

Stage 1: Description of the event • Who? • What? • Where? • When? • Why ?	On my final placement (why) in the accident and emergency department (where) as a third year (when) student nurse (who) I observed a patient having a cardiac arrest (what).
Stage 2: Feelings and thoughts (self-awareness) • What were you thinking? • What were you feeling? • What do you think about it now it is over?	Shock Anxiety Upset Unsure what to do Fear Feeling inadequate
Stage 3: Evaluation • What was good or bad? • What did or did not go so well?	The patient survived. Family were upset. Communication with the family was poor.
Stage 4: Analysis • What went well? • What went wrong or did not turn out how it should have done? • In what way did you or others contribute to this?	Resuscitation process was calm. Communication with family should have been established early and maintained throughout the event. The urgency of the situation took priority.
Stage 5: Conclusion (synthesis) • What could you have done differently? • Have you developed insight into your behaviour?	Recognise that the needs of the family must not be ignored despite the circumstances. More fully aware of the holistic needs of the patient and their family.
Stage 6: Action plan • What would you do in the future?	Allocated a specific member of staff to look after and communicate with the family.

Tips for writing reflectively

- Write about what happened and what you felt – *your feelings*.
- Reflect on what you think about the event, now that it is over – *your thoughts*.
- Write down what other colleagues say about the event – *evidence*.
- Identify what you would do differently – *your actions*.

Activity 5.2 Reflective writing

Now you have a think about a recent event and complete this table.

Stage 1: Description of the event • Who? • What? • Where? • When? • Why?	
Stage 2: Feelings and thoughts (self-awareness) • What were you thinking? • What were you feeling? • What do you think about it now it is over?	
Stage 3: Evaluation • What was good or bad? • What did or did not go so well?	
Stage 4: Analysis • What went well? • What went wrong or did not turn out how it should have done? • In what way did you or others contribute to this?	

Stage 5: Conclusion (synthesis) • What could you have done differently? • Have you developed insight into your behaviour?	
Stage 6: Action plan • What would you do in the future?	

Critical reflective writing

Critical reflection, written or as a thought process, may be helped if you think about asking 'what', 'why' and 'how' questions. The questions you ask yourself for both reflective writing and critical reflective writing are the same. However, to develop and transform your writing from the basic reflective writing style on to a more academic critical writing style you will need to substantiate your claims of acquired knowledge with reference to appropriate literature.

Tips for critical reflective writing

On my final placement (why) in the accident and emergency department (where) as a third year (when) student nurse (who) I observed a patient having a cardiac arrest (what).

• Which authors support or reject my reflections on standards of care?
• What different arguments does the literature put forward?
• What historical and current evidence are these views based upon?
• What other aspects of this experience can be explored through the literature?
• From my own reflections and referring to the literature, what conclusions can be drawn from the experience?
• What is the evidence/theory to support any changes to my practice?

As the Elephant Child said in Rudyard Kipling's *Just So Stories*:

I keep six honest serving men,

They taught me all I knew,

Their names are What and Why and When

And How and Where and Who.

(Kipling 1987)

. . . a cycle of reflection!

How to structure a reflective essay

The structure of a reflective essay will depend upon the reflective model you have chosen to use. It is usually accepted practice to format your essay to reflect the key headings of the model. This also assists you in defining clearly the necessary content to be addressed. Here we provide you with an example of how to structure your reflective essay using Johns's (2000) model. The same principle would apply to whichever model you use.

Example of reflective essay structure

General rules: Contextualise your experience and clearly identify the reflective model being used. Reference the model appropriately and correctly. Identify the need for maintaining confidentiality throughout the essay. Use pseudonyms as appropriate.

Simon was a 67-year-old man who blames himself for his mother's death. Since his mother's death Simon has been diagnosed with severe depression.

Describing an experience significant to the learner (brief introduction)

From the very first day of my placement I had been observing the nurses with Simon on his one-to-one. This means he has to be observed all the time as he is known to be a possible danger to himself or others. Before attempting any interaction with Simon, I read his file which told me his history and why he acts in certain ways. After this I felt a lot more confident going and interacting with Simon.

Identifying personal issues arising from the experience

I have never come across someone who is a known self-harmer so after my first couple of shifts I went home and read up about self-harm. According to Evans and Tippins (2008) self-harm is a way of someone releasing built-up emotions, mainly anger, and is usually caused by depression (Evans and Tippins 2008).

Pinpointing personal intentions

I was slightly apprehensive when I was asking Simon if he wanted to come to the dining room for his dinner. I felt that I should approach Simon smiling and also be very chatty. Simon responded with a very quiet and sober 'ok', which indicated that he wanted to follow me to the dining room. All along he was still being watched on his one-to-one by the nursing assistant.

Empathising with others in the experience

If we didn't use the one-to-one technique then we would not be able to help Simon if he did decide to self-harm again. If Simon did decide to try and self-harm again and he was not being watched he could seriously injure himself or even commit suicide, but also as Simon is on a ward he could upset other patients if they witnessed the incident.

Recognising one's own values and beliefs

I felt nervous about approaching Simon before reading his case notes but after reading them I felt much more confident in approaching Simon. I felt I was watching Simon a lot more as I know with being severely depressed his mood swings fluctuate quickly and randomly.

Linking this experience with previous experiences

I feel that I would be very comfortable dealing with a self-harmer now and realise conversation is a great way to communicate with them and not to be apprehensive of them. I will always remember that reading through case notes and a patient's file is a great way to gain knowledge and understanding of a patient at first, without meeting them.

Creating new options for future behaviour

The experience has made me realise there are many different ways to talk and communicate with people. Reading case notes is a great way to help get an insight to the patient's problems.

Looking at ways to improve working with patients, families, and staff in order to meet patients' needs

As Simon is a known depressive it's hard to tell what his true feeling and thoughts were but after spending a few days with slight conversation I gathered Simon was fond of Johnny Cash so we had a good few conversations about Johnny Cash and some other musicians. This seemed to cheer Simon up a lot and even laughing and joking now and again.

Conclusion

Reflective practice is important as health and social care professionals are responsible for providing care to the best of their ability to patients, families and carers. They are personally accountable for actions and omissions in their practice and must always be able to justify their decisions. You need to reflect on your knowledge, skills and behaviour to ensure you are able to meet the standards defined by your professional regulatory body.

Reflective practice has been identified as a necessary tool for health and social care students to recognise their own strengths and weaknesses. It is a method of being aware as a practitioner of yourself and your skills and abilities and to acknowledge your strengths and identify your weakness.

Hints and tips

- Use a reflective model to support the process of reflection.
- Familiarise yourself with your module outcomes at the start of each academic year, to ensure you are writing at the correct academic level.
- Descriptive writing should offer the reader a sense as if they were there themselves.
- Writing an explanation should provide evidence that you understand something, and include details on concepts, processes and procedures, as well as relationships.
- Ensure written arguments are believable and support any conclusion being made.

- Remember that analysis involves assessing the strengths and weaknesses of each premise and any claim itself.
- Where you are asked to evaluate, use questions such as: How well did it work? How do we know? What needs to change? What will I do differently?
- Be aware that synthesis involves discussing several viewpoints, showing your understanding of them, to the point where you are able to offer a fresh perspective on the subject and make new connections.

References

Dewey, J. (1997) *How We Think.* Mineola, NY: Dover Publications.

Evans, C. and Tippins, E. (2008) *Foundations of Nursing: An Integrated Approach.* Maidenhead: McGraw-Hill.

Gibbs, G. (1988) *Learning by Doing: A Guide to Teaching and Learning Methods.* Oxford: Further Education Unit, Oxford Brookes University.

Jasper, M. (2003) *Beginning Reflective Practice. Foundations in Nursing and Health Care.* Cheltenham: Nelson Thornes.

Johns, C. (2000) *Becoming a Reflective Practitioner: A Reflective and Holistic Approach to Clinical Nursing, Practice Development and Clinical Supervision.* Oxford: Blackwell.

Kipling, R. (1987) *Just So Stories.* London: Penguin (first published 1902).

Kolb. D. (1985) *Learning Style Inventory: Self Scoring Inventory and Interpretation Booklet.* Boston, MA: McBer.

Moon, J. (2004) *A Handbook of Reflective and Experiential Learning.* London: Routledge Falmer.

Schön, D. A. (1987) *Educating the Reflective Practitioner: Toward a New Design for Teaching and Learning in the Professions.* San Francisco: Jossey-Bass.

Schön, D. A. (1995) *The Reflective Practitioner: How Professionals Think in Action.* San Francisco: Basic Books.

Somerville, D. and Keeling, J. (2004) A practical approach to promote reflective practice within nursing, *Nursing Times,* 100(12): 42.

6

Writing for practice

Pat Talbot

This chapter explores the following topics:

- How is writing for practice different from academic writing?
- Why is it important that records are well written?
- What is a record?
- What should be recorded?
- How should the information be recorded?
- Confidentiality, access and disclosure
- What role do records have in complaints and legal claims?
- Writing a report or statement

Introduction

You will need to write every day as part of your professional role, in order to formulate your understanding of situations, develop action plans and care plans, communicate with other professionals and agencies, and to record that you have carried out the practice for which you are accountable. Writing for practice may differ in terms of the specific purpose, format or regulation in relation to the professional role.

This chapter aims to set out general principles and give examples or make practical suggestions related to specific disciplines. Consequently, some of the language or applications may relate more to one professional role than another. However, the information is useful to all health and social care professionals. When you are asked to document an assessment or intervention in practice, it can seem daunting, but you have a mentor or practice educator who can advise you and supervise your record keeping.

Once qualified, you are accountable for your practice, and all records can be scrutinised as part of any review of care or legal case, even if you are not directly involved. Records are important because they provide a framework for your assessment, decisions, referrals and interventions in practice, as well as providing an audit trail of your actions and your reasons.

This chapter examines the skills you need for writing in practice. As with all writing, you will decide what points you need to make and the order in which to make them so that they lead to a logical conclusion. You will still need to present your writing so that it makes sense. However, key differences include consideration of who will read your records, what purpose they will be used for, the legal implications of what you write and ensuring that your writing is clear, concise and accessible. While writing for an academic audience is about demonstrating knowledge and depth of understanding, writing for practice colleagues, service users and lay audiences is about providing them with the information they need to understand situations and make decisions, often with limited time.

This chapter reviews the skills you need to enable you to keep safe and effective service user records. It explains the importance of clear and accurate record keeping and gives you some hints on what you should record, and how to write and keep records that meet current guidelines. The management of electronic records and communication in writing is discussed, along with some basic guidelines to maintaining confidentiality across different media. Report writing is considered in some depth, as you may need to write reports about service users, critical incidents or practice issues, which require complex evaluation of a variety of factors, including ethico-legal considerations. You might also like to refer to Chapter 5 on reflective writing.

How is writing for practice different from academic writing?

Writing for practice has several key differences with academic writing:

- You are writing for a different audience (this might include the service user and their family, and other health or social care professionals, the police, teachers or professionals from other agencies) so your writing style needs to be clear and understandable.

- You are not writing in order to demonstrate you academic ability, but to present information effectively – you need to write concisely and focus on the key points.
- In practice, information might need to be provided in order to facilitate referrals or transfers of patients or service users.
- You may be required to recommend a plan of care or intervention based on your assessment of a social situation, physical problem or psychological need – ensure your assessment is written as objectively as possible, using available tools and neutral language.
- The content will often consist of a record of events and will be factual in nature, rather than theoretical. Theoretical concepts might underpin the content, but will not normally be included in a report or record.
- Your records and reports might be reviewed in a legal setting, so decide what you must include in order to justify your actions and provide essential information for colleagues. This is particularly relevant for social workers writing court reports, where the primary purpose is to provide evidence on which the court can make decisions. Clear communication is necessary for evaluation of practice and review of critical incidents – a lack of documentation suggests that care has not been given.

Activity 6.1 Academic writing and writing/or practice

From the examples below, choose which you think is in 'academic' or 'writing for practice' style.

1 John did not play with the toys or engage with any of the adults in the room, but sat quietly rocking in the corner.
2 According to Smythe (2012) pets can form part of a therapeutic environment. However, Jones (2013) would argue that the presence of pets in the environment can offer no benefit and may have negative health implications.
3 The ethical framework for keeping written records in social work is complex, and requires consideration of the purpose for which they are written, as well as the rights of the individuals concerned and the legal context of the situation (Brown 2014).
4 Factors which contributed to the incident included an inappropriate skill mix on the ward, an unexpected emergency admission and a high ratio of patients with complex needs.

Activity 6.1 feedback

The first statement is an example of writing for practice – it is a record of observed behaviour that could be relevant to an opinion about the care needs of a child. The second statement is an example of academic writing – it is referenced and presents two contrasting viewpoints. The third statement is an example of a general, introductory statement in academic writing, a summary of current knowledge. The fourth statement is an example of writing for practice – its purpose is to present an expert opinion on events to identify cause and improve future practice.

Why is it important that records are well written?

The Nursing and Midwifery Council (NMC) states: 'Good record keeping is an integral part of nursing and midwifery practice, and is essential to the provision of safe and effective care. It is not an optional extra to be fitted in if circumstances allow' (2009: 1). The Health and Care Professions Council (HCPC, 2012) sets out 12 standards for social work practice, including being 'able to communicate effectively' (p. 11) and being 'able to maintain records appropriately' (p. 12). In a review of child protection services following the death of Baby Peter, the standard of record keeping across all services was found to be inconsistent and poor by the Joint Area Review of Haringey Children's Services Authority Area (Ofsted/Healthcare Commission/HM Inspectorate of Constabulary 2008). Recommendations included monitoring the quality of case files and ensuring accountability for case work decisions by all staff.

Record keeping is central to accountability. If a professional does not keep good records of their assessments, decisions, actions and evaluations in practice, they do not show awareness of their accountability for decisions to act or not to act. Clearly, when developing your knowledge for writing in practice, as well as understanding the specific guidelines for practice, you would need to document specific observations and concerns, and make recommendations. Not only does good record keeping provide the basis for interventions and allow practice to be monitored, it also helps you to identify any further information you need to make a decision, and clarifies your position so that you can make more rational, evidence-based judgements.

Good record keeping can ensure quality care for service users by:

• providing effective communication between the multiprofessional team.

- ensuring continuity of care
- assisting in the detection of risks and/or complications
- enabling professionals to make effective and safe decisions
- facilitating collaboration between service user and professional (Parr 2013).

Good records can also benefit learners in the organisation by:

- demonstrating how care decisions have been made.

Effective records can also support the organisation quality agenda by:

- ensuring that there is evidence of the care provided
- providing information for practice audit, researchers and resource allocation
- providing information to help address complaints or legal requirements.

(Nursing and Midwifery Council, 2009)

Poor record keeping can result in tests or procedures having to be repeated and services users having to answer the same questions repeatedly (Medical Protection Society 2008).

Activity 6.2 Record keeping

Issues around record keeping are amongst the top three reasons for people to appear before the Fitness to Practice Panel of the NMC.

Go to the NMC website http://www.nmc-uk.org

Click on 'Hearings' and look at the details of some of the recent proceedings of the Fitness to Practice Panel. What kind of failures in record keeping have contributed to the cases that you have examined?

The Health and Care Professions Council also holds fitness for practice hearings and their website can be found at http://www.hcpc-uk.org/

Activity 6.2 feedback

You might have found some cases where record keeping and writing skills (or lack of them) might have played a part. However, you are more likely to find that falsification of records is an area that is taken very seriously by the NMC. HCPC fitness for practice hearings generally relate to ethical behaviour, but inquiries into social work failings often comment on poor documentation.

There is evidence that while nurses do view documentation as important, they do not always keep adequate records and they do not always use records to inform their practice (Law et al. 2010). In all health and social care disciplines, records should be used as a basis for decision making, as well as a record of care given, and used to evaluate the care given in a continuous cycle. They should be helpful to all practitioners, promoting thoughtful and integrated care, not just treated as a task at the end of the day's work.

What is a record?

The same principles are applied to all types of records, however they are held. Most records are written records.

A record might consist of:

- Case diaries
- Case files
- Computerised records
- Court statements
- Court reports
- E-mails
- Handwritten notes
- Letters
- Minutes of professional meetings
- Photographs or videos
- Police referrals
- Printouts from electronic monitors
- Recorded telephone conversations (as in NHS Direct)
- Referrals to other professionals or agencies
- Reports for panels or safeguarding agencies
- Reports or statements regarding events
- Text messages
- X rays

(National Midwifery Council 2009;
Rai and Lillis 2009; Wood 2010)

Any document that is requested by a court of law becomes a legal document (Dimond 2008). So when you write in any service user record, it could be examined in court.

What should be recorded?

Full and complete record keeping will support effective and well-planned care. The NMC (2009) identifies that we have a duty to make sure that co-workers have the information they need in order to provide safe and effective care. If legal claims do occur, they are often related to incomplete or inadequate record keeping (Wood 2010). The HCPC require social workers 'to demonstrate effective and appropriate skills in communicating advice, instruction, information and professional opinion to colleagues, service users and carers' (Health and Care Professions Council, 2012: 9) and 'keep accurate, comprehensive and comprehensible records in accordance with applicable legislation, protocols and guidelines' (Health and Care Professions Council, 2012: 12). Where emotive and contentious issues are commonplace, good record keeping avoids confusion, provides evidence to support practice and prevents misinterpretation. Written records allow professionals to provide a chronological, fact-based analysis of a situation in order to inform practice, promote accountability and meet legal requirements (Parr 2013).

The updated *Essence of Care* document (Department of Health 2010), which applies to health and social care, identifies a benchmark for best practice: 'People's care records demonstrate that their care is evidence based' (p. 12). They particularly stress that an explanation is required if the care given is not evidence based. They also suggest that staff need to agree on a format for evidence-based documentation. You need to record the following aspects of care:

- A statement of the situation of the service user at the beginning of each care episode or interview, including records of observations, assessments and reviews. Include information that may influence the care you provide.
- Treatment and care given (not just the plan of care, but also a record that the care was delivered) as well as advice offered and agreed decisions, or where care interventions are offered but rejected.
- Advice given to the service user or carers, even on the telephone (Glasper 2011).

- Referrals to other health and social care professionals or other services.
- Risk assessments and strategies put in place to minimise risk.

Activity 6.3 Which items should you record?

You are caring for Miss Davenport, an elderly lady who is in a very confused state. Her neighbour comes in to visit and tells you the following:

- Miss Davenport is devoted to her two cats, which the neighbour is currently feeding.
- She has a son in America and she provides a telephone number for him.
- She has had several falls over the last few months.
- Miss Davenport has told her neighbour that she is frightened of doctors.
- She does not drink tea or coffee.

Which items would you record?

You are caring for Mr Wedgwood, a 40-year-old man with an intellectual disability, who lived with his mother until her death a few days ago. He is now living alone. You make a home visit to assess his social care needs and observe the following:

- Mr Wedgwood appears clean and well dressed; the house is clean and tidy.
- Mr Wedgwood tells you that he is very sad.
- Mr Wedgwood does not know where to get money from for the housekeeping and will run out of food and essentials within the next two days.
- Mr Wedgwood tells you he does not know about any relatives but he has friends at the local day services centre and he does voluntary work at a local animal charity.
- Mr Wedgwood shows you a drawer that his mother told him to open if she was not there to look after him. You find a copy of the will, bank books and other legal documents.
- Mr Wedgwood has looked after himself for short periods in the past when his mum has had short holidays with a friend, and recently when she was in hospital.

Which items would you record?

Activity 6.3 feedback

Mrs Davenport – All these items should be recorded – they all have relevance to her care.

Mr Wedgwood – Again, all of these items should be recorded, as well as where the documentation was, the observations you made about Mr Wedgwood's psychological well-being and coping strategies, the advice you gave Mr Wedgwood, your professional opinion as to the services Mr Wedgwood will require, and your action plan and referrals.

How should the information be recorded?

Effective record keeping will provide an audit trail, which demonstrates the service user journey. There is a duty to ensure that records meet the standard identified in the CIA mnemonic (Glasper 2011):

- Clear
- Intelligible
- Accurate.

The Nursing and Midwifery Council (2009) and Aberdeen City Council/Robert Gordon University (2010) provide guidance on the process of safe and effective record keeping. The following content has been informed by their work and that of other authors. The points made are applicable to all health and social care professional records.

What to record and what not to record

Avoid transcribing technical information, such as information on prescribed medication. Where an original document exists and can be accessed and referred to, it is preferable to do so, particularly when it is the primary legal record. The more times that information is transcribed, the more chances there are for errors. If you wanted to record that a medication was not effective so you asked for a review, you could record this and explain that the dosage or frequency was increased, or the administration method altered or the drug changed or another drug added, and refer the reader to the record. Drug prescription sheets can be printed out if a permanent, hard copy is required to show the changes made. In social work, case records provide a central point to link together e-mails between other agencies, factual information, service user statements and other documents, but it is important to identify and discuss only the key points of these. For example, document why a referral was made, its purpose and its expected outcome, referring the reader to the actual document for further detail. This is necessary to maintain the integrity of your narrative: your statement of what the service user's situation is; what problems there are and why intervention is required; and what the goal of social care is (Healy and Mulholland 2007). Unnecessary detail makes the record more difficult and time consuming to read, and it can detract from the important points, obscuring your reasoning, actions and conclusions.

Make sure you only record relevant and factual information. Do not include speculation and personal opinions. In social work, decisions will be based on observation, assessment, protocol and judgements involving the best interests of the vulnerable and protection of society. They are often complex and it is important that they are given due consideration that is reflected in the documentation. You are required to make judgements about needs and interventions, developing your opinions through careful consideration of relevant factors, but it is important to separate facts from opinions (Healy and Mulholland 2007), so that colleagues and others can use that information appropriately. Writing is a tool for thinking and helps you to make sense of the care situations that you encounter, and the decisions you need to make. Whatever discipline you practise within, good record keeping is not just a record of what you have done, it is an aid to coherent thinking about the person's needs, care planning and evaluation of care.

Activity 6.4

Identify what is wrong with the following record:

> Mrs Jones was found on the toilet floor. She must have slipped, as the floor was wet. She sustained a fracture to her wrist and she is now resting in bed.

What additional information should be included?
    Identify what is wrong with the following record:

> Mr Smith was living in an untidy house and was unable to care for himself. He lives alone and will therefore need a package of services.

What additional information should be included?

Activity 6.4 feedback

1 Mrs Jones needs to be more clearly identified.
2 Who found Mrs Jones?
3 Avoid assumptions regarding the wet floors, unless Mrs Jones has stated that she slipped.
4 More detail regarding the action taken – for example, was a doctor called for Mrs. Jones, name of doctor, action taken. Was documentation completed?
5 Mr Smith needs to be more clearly identified and basic demographic information is needed.
6 An objective description of Mr. Smith's living environment is needed as what is untidy to one person could be homely to another
7 What does Mr. Smith say about his problems, needs and preferred outcomes?
8 Give the assessment information to support the contention that Mr Smith was unable to care for himself independently. What was he able to do, and what was he not able to do? Be specific in order to identify problems and plan appropriate service provision and referrals.
9 What informal support and resources does Mr Smith have?
10 What specific interventions would help Mr. Smith and why? Record any referrals or interventions you instigated.

Writing clearly

First, handwritten records need to be clear and legible. The record should be signed with the name of the person and their role printed alongside. In some settings, records made by students will need to be countersigned (Dimond 2008). Records may need to be photocopied or scanned in the future, so a black pen is advised (Wood 2010). Pencil should never be used. Many health and social care professionals make temporary notes to be formally recorded later, but Glasper (2011) believes that this is best avoided. He suggests that notes of this type need to be formalised and that some believe that the original should be preserved. Ensure that if you write any temporary notes, for example, of a telephone conversation, keep them in the case file to support your case notes. Photographs that are not directly related to the clinical needs of the service user should not be used (Nursing and Midwifery Council, 2009).

Writing accurately

When documenting care, you should ensure that information which identifies the service user (e.g. date of birth) is correct. All records need to be timed (with the 24-hour clock) and dated – you should complete records as soon as possible after the event. Notes made at the time are more likely to be accurate, and by making notes at the time you are ensuring that the record is written. Write the record so that its meaning is clear. It is easy to use meaningless phrases such as 'Had a good day.' This could have a variety of meanings, as identified by Dimond (2008), which might include 'She has been pain free' or 'She has walked to the day room' or 'She has spent the day sleeping.'

Writing intelligibly

Try to make sure that you record information in chronological order, as this helps the reader to locate information and to follow events. Records should never be altered or destroyed without permission. However, if you need to amend a record, then you must sign and date the alteration, giving your name and job title. They must ensure that both the original and the new record can be clearly seen (Nursing and Midwifery Council 2009). This can be done by placing a line through the old record, whilst still allowing the original to be read. Do not use correction fluid. Amendments to records held electronically can be colour coded so that, for example, first amendments can appear in red (Glasper 2011). In order to maintain the clarity of records, Glasper (2011) suggests using a rule which he calls 'No ELBOW'. This means:

- No Erasing.
- No Leaves, or pages to be removed.
- No Blank spaces – put a line through spaces to ensure that additions are not made.
- No Overwriting to ensure that amendments are clear.
- No Writing in margins – they should be left clear for times and dates for the entry.

Where possible, involve service users and/or their carers in the process of record keeping. (Nursing and Midwifery Council 2009) This can help ensure that the services user's viewpoint is represented in the record of care. In social work, by discussing problems with service users prior to writing up case notes, it allows them to contribute towards an understanding of their needs. It aids the service user in clarifying their understanding of the situation so that they can identify which problems they see as priorities; and it allows them to understand the role of the social worker and understand how the social worker can help them (Healy and Mulholland 2007).

Using abbreviations

Try to avoid the use of abbreviations as they could alter the meaning of the record. The Royal College of Nursing (2010a) uses the phrase 'short forms' to include 'abbreviations, acronyms, initialisations and any other form of text reduction' (p. 2). They believe that 'short forms' should be avoided. This is in agreement with the Nursing and Midwifery Council (2009) However, the Royal College of Nursing (2010a) acknowledges that some abbreviations are so commonly used in society that the use of the full term could cause confusion. They cite examples such as 'am', 'pm' and 'NHS' and propose that there should be national agreement on a standard list of acceptable abbreviations. The use of a wide variety of non-standardised abbreviations by health professionals can lead to confusion.

Activity 6.5 Abbreviations

What might the following abbreviations mean?

1 Ca
2 pt
3 CP
4 MS

Dimond (2008)

Activity 6.5 feedback

1 Cancer or calcium?
2 Patient, physiotherapist or part time?
3 Cerebral palsy or chartered physiotherapist?
4 Multiple sclerosis or mitral stenosis?

Social work uses acronyms to identify a wide variety of acts, agencies, service user situations and forms. These are generally standardised within local policy. However, it is good practice to write out an acronym in full the first time it is used within a case file, to avoid confusion. Guidance on the matter of abbreviations can be conflicting (Royal College of Nursing 2010) as the Department of Health (2010) suggests that authorised abbreviations are acceptable. If abbreviations are to be used they should be explained, as should the use of jargon. As a general guide, you should write so that a lay person in a different profession could understand your writing.

Recording results

When you are working in health settings, you should be aware of the system used for receiving and recording results. They are often received and held electronically, but there should be a back-up system in place to cover in the event of a system failure. When you need to record results, local and national protocols should be followed and care taken in relation to recording numerical information, particularly in relation to decimal points. The information should be recorded immediately in an appropriate section of the person's records.

Activity 6.7 Telephone communication

What do you think might go wrong when results are communicated by telephone? Try to identify three possible problems that might occur when you are writing down results that are given over the telephone.

1
2
3

Activity 6.7 feedback

1 It is difficult to identify the person who is speaking.
2 Information may be misheard.
3 It is difficult to maintain confidentiality.

A telephone call can result in notes being taken on scraps of paper or sticky notes which can be misplaced.

Writing electronic records

Activity 6.8 Electronic records

Consider how you might feel about electronic records being kept about you or your family. What issues might you be concerned about?

Activity 6.8 feedback

You might be concerned about:

- Who can access the records
- Might records be altered, or even lost?
- Might the records be used a way that you would not be happy with?

Many services now use electronic record systems. The Royal College of Nursing (2010b) states that electronic records should present a true reflection of the nursing care that is planned and provided. They suggest this can be achieved by developing systems that are able to record nursing practice in a way which reflects the nursing process. They point out that this should include the views and expectations of the service user and communications with the service user and others. They also believe that nursing information needs to be recorded in a structured format with a national standardised terminology, although they support the use of free text to provide the full picture. It is suggested that those using electronic records should be guided by the acronym SAFER:

S: Conform to STANDARDS.

A: Are ACCEPTABLE to patients, clients, carers and health care workers.

F: FIT for purpose and practice.

E: Are supported by EVIDENCE.

R: Are RISK MANAGED.

Guidance on record keeping for social work professionals by Aberdeen City Council and Robert Gordon University (2010) provides some useful points about electronic communication referred to in this section. Text messaging may be used in social care particularly, in order to improve communication with service users. However, for your own protection, do not use personal mobile telephones, and to maintain confidentiality there should be a pin code for access to the telephone, and you should report the loss or theft of the telephone to the police immediately. Any text messages sent or received should be recorded in the case file, as they are a service user contact.

When you send e-mails, they are likely to be in the public domain indefinitely, so take them as seriously as any other form or record, using professional language such as 'Dear Mr Jones' rather than 'Hi John', for example. Avoid abbreviations, but write concisely because people expect to be able to respond to e-mails promptly. Most importantly, ensure that your reader knows exactly who you are, what position you hold, what organisation you work for and how to contact you. Put the subject matter of your e-mail in the subject box, but avoid using individuals' names. Remember that once you have sent your e-mail other people may forward it, or it may be used in an audit or legal process, so maintain your professional ethical and writing standards.

You should never completely delete any information from an electronic record. However, most systems are able to keep an audit trail of any changes, in terms of what was changed and who made the changes and when (Royal College of Nursing, 2010c). Make sure that you shut down computers after use and never share your password (Wood 2009), and ensure that your computer is password encrypted and that you log off even if leaving the computer for a short time (Aberdeen City Council and Robert Gordon University 2010). Records that are held on removable media such as disks, laptops, handheld computers and memory sticks must be encrypted (Department of Health 2010) in order to protect the confidentiality of your service users.

Regarding abbreviations, the Royal College of Nursing (2010a) reminds us that a computerised system can allow abbreviations to be entered which the computer will then display in its full form. However, some systems may only provide a small space for data entry, and the system may generate a short form to fit the space.

Tips for writing electronic records

When writing records on an electronic system you need to remember the following:

- Familiarise yourself with the system – this might involve attending a training session.
- Keep passwords safe and do not share them with others.
- Record all relevant information, just as in a paper based system.
- Remember that, just as with paper records, service users, families and other health care workers may access the information that you have recorded.
- Do not walk away from the screen, allowing others to view the information.
- Never take information away with you on a disk or memory stick.

Confidentiality, access and disclosure

The public are now more aware of their right to access care records. The *Essence of Care* document (Department of Health 2010) identifies a benchmark for good practice as: 'People are able to access their care records in a format that meets their needs' (p. 9). A service can indicate good practice in this area by demonstrating that, for example, service users have a copy of their care plan (where appropriate) or that they are promoting awareness of the right to access records. Consider this right of access when you enter information into any system, especially in relation to the use of clear, understandable language. If service users do not routinely have access to their records, you should be aware of local policies on this. You should only access records that are relevant to a service user in your care, in order to protect the confidentiality of service users.

What role do records have in complaints and legal claims?

It is important to remember that negligence claims can be made years after the episode of care, when the staff involved may not recall the events or may no longer be employed in the area. When a claim is to be made, the first thing that the claimant or their representative will ask for will be the care records. The standard of care provided will be judged by the quality of the record keeping. If records are incomplete or carelessly written, then the courts will work on the assumption that this reflects poor care. If care was not documented, it can be inferred that it was not carried out. The strongest evidence in a court of law is the service user record (Medical Protection Society 2008)

Some relevant legislation

The Data Protection Act 1998 applies to the processing of personal information in general which is held manually or on computer. Some principles of the Act are listed in Table 6.1, with their implications for health and social care professionals, and how you write about service users.

Table 6.1 Data Protection Act – some basic principles

Principle from the Data Protection Act	Implications when writing and record keeping
Personal data must be processed in a way that is compatible with the purpose for which it was obtained.	Remember that the content of what you write is only to be used to provide safe and effective care for the service user.
Personal data should be adequate, relevant and not excessive.	Confine yourself to only what is needed, but remember the value of a holistic approach as demonstrated in Activity 6.3.
Information should be correct and up to date.	Ensure that personal details are correct and that you update records regularly and in 'real time'.
Information should be protected from loss, damage or unauthorised processing.	Ensure that you are familiar with the system. Never transfer data unless to a secure system.

Writing a report or statement

Under some circumstances you may be asked to write a report or statement. This might consist of a report on an incident, the progress of a service user for a review or the current condition of a service user in order to aid transfer to another service. A statement might be required for legal purposes such as criminal, civil, coroner's or tribunal proceedings. You should consider the following:

• Who will read the report?
• What type of information is required?
• How is the information to be presented and organised?

Social work court reports are used to inform decisions about child protection. The credibility of your report will be based on your previous use of your records to track and inform your practice, as well as your ability to present your findings clearly. They will invariably have been scrutinised by the appropriate legal advisor for the local authority, although you are likely to be questioned as a witness in care proceedings and so need to be able to base your verbal testimony on what has been written in your report. They should include:

- a factual outline of events, behaviour and observations
- analysis, evaluation and an assessment of the facts leading to a professional understanding of them
- an evidence-based recommendation with an action plan to support it (Aberdeen City Council and Robert Gordon University 2010).

Court reports should be literate; concise; understandable; distinguish between fact, analysis and opinion; give a rationale for decisions and opinions (Keen et al. 2010).

Where you are completing an incident report form, then you should follow the policy of the service provider. This will probably include the completion of the organisation's documentation which will include an accident or incident form, an accident or incident logbook, the service user's personal record and possible a daily report/communication book (Ashurst 2007). Before compiling the report you may need to speak to everyone involved to gain a clear understanding of both what led up to the event and the event itself. It may be appropriate for witnesses to write their own account of the incident (Ashurst 2007). The report should provide details of the events before the incident, the incident itself and events which followed (Ashurst 2007).

Points to include in your report:

- Clearly identify the service user and others involved.
- Date and time of incident.
- Your full name, position and role.
- The nature and severity of the event.
- How the service user was affected.
- What action was taken.
- The information that was given to the service user.
- Others involved in events (if they have provided statements they should accompany the report).
- Others who have been informed of events.
- Other statements or documents should be attached (Ashurst 2007; Dimond 2008; Medical Protection Society 2008).

When you write a report it is important to ensure that your writing is well organised and that there is an effective 'flow' to the text. Iyer (2010) gives some useful advice on how to achieve this:

- Create a structure for your work that is logical – avoid repetition and do not ramble. The most important aspect of the report is usually to present factually accurate information in an easy to follow format.
- Each paragraph should cover a single topic.
- Keep paragraphs short – this is easier on the eye for the reader.
- Use transitions to help the reader. These can demonstrate the sequence of events (e.g. 'first', 'next', 'finally') or they can indicate a contrast (e.g. 'instead').
- Avoid very long sentences – the reader is likely to find it difficult to follow the meaning of the sentence. However, try to vary the sentence length so that you do not use a series of very short sentences.
- Try to use words that will be familiar to the reader.
- Avoid using more words than necessary; for example, 'in the event that' can be replaced by 'if'.
- When starting a paragraph always refer to the service user by name, rather than using 'he' or 'she'. However, the following sentence could begin with 'he' or 'she'. For example: 'Mr Price was involved in a fight in the town centre. He was brought to accident and emergency by a friend.'
- Avoid words that add nothing to the meaning such as 'obviously', 'generally' and 'actually'.
- Use terminology in a consistent way. For example, do not switch between 'service user' and 'client'.
- If time allows, set the report aside and go back to it later to check and edit the document. Careful proofreading will avoid errors that might detract from the effectiveness of the document. Reading out loud can help to identify errors or sentences that are poorly constructed. If confidentiality allows, ask another person to check the report for clarity.

Activity 6.9 Incident report

Look at the following report, prepared by the person in charge. How many ways of improving this report can you identify?

It all started on Sunday morning when I went upstairs with Jenny Smith and Sally Saunders. John Delgado had told me

> *that Sally Saunders had been trying to upset Jenny Smith because she had taken her magazine. Jenny came out of her room with a magazine. She hit her and as she ran she fell over. A huge lump came up on the side of her head. She went into her room and started to throw things about. Graham Mellor got upset, saying that she should not be allowed to make all this noise and he hit her with his walking frame. Then he left.*

Activity 6.9 feedback

- Where did the event take place?
- The report lacks dates and times.
- Were the people in a place where someone had a duty of care?
- Who witnessed the events – were any other staff present?
- The individuals named have not been identified.
- The sentence structure used leaves the reader unsure regarding who took each of the actions. There is too much use of 'she'.
- More detail needed regarding the fall – was it caused by anything in particular?
- More detail regarding the 'huge lump' – where was the swelling and how large was it? Were there any other effects of the fall? What action was taken regarding the injury?
- More details needed regarding the walking frame. Where was she hit? Were there any injuries, and if so what was done about them?
- Where did Graham Mellor go after the incident?
- What was done after the incident regarding documentation or follow up?

Conclusion

This chapter has identified the skills and knowledge needed for writing in practice. The emphasis is on recording useful information in a way that can be understood by colleagues and service users, enabling events to be understood, evidence-based conclusions to be reached and appropriate professional and legal decisions to be made. Some pertinent legal issues around what should be recorded, how it should be recorded and what counts as a record have been highlighted. Until you have qualified, your records should be monitored and countersigned by a registered practitioner, so take that opportunity to seek advice on how to improve your practice writing skills. Record keeping is essential for professional practice, so developing these skills is fundamental to your future practice. If in doubt, always check with a senior colleague, as documentation is the most visible aspect of professional practice for which we are all held accountable.

Hints and tips

- Write the record as close as possible to the events you are writing about.
- Present information within a clear and logical structure.
- Use language suitable for the reader, but as a general rule it should be simple and direct.
- Avoid writing in a style that is judgemental and stick to the facts.
- The care records and reports that you write might be accessed by service users or their families.
- Be aware of legal requirements and national and local guidelines that might affect what and how you write.
- Where your opinion is required, make sure it is supported by a clear analysis of the facts and identification of the theoretical underpinning to your conclusions – differentiate between fact and opinion.

References

Aberdeen City Council and Robert Gordon University (2010) *Professional Writing Guidance Booklet for Social Work Practitioners* (2nd edn). http://ebookbrowse.com/professional-writing-guidance-booklet-edition-2-pdf-d53638280.

Ashurst, A. (2007) Writing an accident or incident report, *Nursing and Residential Care*, 9(8): 381–383.

Department of Health (2010) *Essence of Care 2010: Benchmarks for Record Keeping*. London: The Stationery Office.

Dimond, B. (2008) *Legal Aspects of Nursing* (5th edn). Harlow: Pearson.

Glasper, A. (2011) Improving record keeping: important lessons for nurses, *British Journal of Nursing*, 20(14): 886–887.

Health and Care Professions Council (HCPC, 2012) *Standards of Proficiency: Social Workers in England*. London: Health and Care Professions Council.

Healy, K. and Mulholland, J. (2007) *Writing Skills for Social Workers*. London: Sage.

Iyer, P. (2010) Sharpen your writing skills: Part 2, *Journal of Legal Nurse Consulting*, 21(3): 11–13.

Keen, S., Gray, I., Parker, J., Galpin, D. and Brown, K. (2010) *Newly-Qualified Social Workers: A Handbook for Practice*. Exeter: Learning Matters.

Law, L., Akroyd, K. and Burke, L. (2010) Improving nurse documentation and record keeping in stoma care, *British Journal of Nursing*, 19(21): 1328–1332.

Medical Protection Society (2008*) Introducing Clinical Risk Management. A Trainer's Resource. Module 2 – Patients' Records*. London: Medical Protection Society.

Nursing and Midwifery Council (NMC, 2009) *Record Keeping: Guidance for Nurses and Midwives*. London: Nursing and Midwifery Council.

Ofsted/Healthcare Commission/HM Inspectorate of Constabulary (2008) *Joint Area Review: Haringey Children's Services Authority Area*. www.education. gov.uk/publications/standard/publicationDetail/Page1/HARINGEY-REVIEW.

Parr, T. (2013) Record keeping, in A., Worsley, T., Mann, A. Olsen and E. Mason-Whitehead, *Key Concepts in Social Work Practice*. London: Sage.

Pirie, S. (2011) Documentation and record keeping, *Journal of Perioperative Practice*, 21(1): 22–27.

Rai, L. and Lillis, T. (2009) *Getting it Right/Write. Exploring Professional Writing in Social Work*. Open University: www.open.ac.uk/opencetl/files/opencetl/file/ecms/web-content/Rai-and-Lillis-(2009)-Getting-it-right-write-An-exploration-of-professional-social-work-writing-Final-project-report-PBPL-paper-46.pdf.

Royal College of Nursing (2010a) *Abbreviations and Other Short Forms in Patient/Client Records*. London: Royal College of Nursing.

Royal College of Nursing (2010b) *Nursing Content of eHealth Records*. London: Royal College of Nursing.

Royal College of Nursing (2010c) *Consent to Create, Amend, Access and Share eHealth Records*. London: Royal College of Nursing.

Wood, S. (2010) Effective record-keeping, *Practice Nurse*, 39(4): 20–23.

7

Presenting your writing in different formats

Victoria Ridgway and June Keeling

This chapter explores the following topics:

- Essays
- Oral presentations/examinations
- Poster presentation
- Dissertation structuring and writing
- Portfolio development
- Writing for publication

Introduction

Traditionally, students in higher education (HE) were assessed by exams, these being processes in which you would have been required to answer a list of questions from an unseen paper. However, higher education institutes have become increasingly innovative at assessing your knowledge, and now you will be asked to present your work for assessment in a variety of formats. This approach has many advantages over the traditional exam method of assessment, as you may have experienced 'exam nerves' and produced substandard work when in the exam setting. You may now be assessed by using a variety of methods which enable you to use your creativity whilst still providing adequate evidence of achieving the required level to pass. Therefore, this chapter presents many of the different formats that may be used to assess your progression in higher education. Each type of assessment is illustrated, and includes key tips for success to guide you away from the common pitfalls.

We begin the chapter by exploring the use of the traditional written examination in the form of an essay. Oral presentations and examinations may be used to assess your knowledge throughout your programme of study in health and social care. These are probing exams, in that they enable examiners to easily assess your knowledge. Poster presentations are increasingly used to assess your overall knowledge of a system or process. This chapter also includes tips on how to construct a poster and how to present your work clearly.

Your final piece of work as both an undergraduate and postgraduate student may be a dissertation. This is also usually the largest piece of work you will complete. This chapter addresses two key areas to consider in a dissertation: how you feel towards developing a dissertation and how to write a dissertation.

Towards the end of your programme of study, you may be required to assemble a portfolio, a record of your acquired skills and knowledge to date. The construction and content of your portfolio are crucial to showcase yourself at any interview, and provide documentary evidence of how you fulfil your professional role. We have included advice and useful tips on how to construct and write a portfolio.

Finally, you may be offered the opportunity to develop one of your assignments for publication. This is the final product of writing and one that should be pursued if an opportunity arises. This chapter concludes with a section on writing for publication. Each section of the chapter will guide you on how to produce each of these formats to enhance the quality of your submitted work.

Essays

We start this chapter by exploring easy writing, as essays are the most common form of academic assessment. They are often used throughout education, at different levels from primary school through to university courses, to assess the student's knowledge and application to a subject. Despite the many repetitions of this process of writing essays, students still experience anxiety when writing them. Therefore in this section of the chapter we provide an overview of the process of writing an essay, breaking it down into bite-sized chunks to enable the student to progress through each step with ease.

Six steps to success

1 *Research.* The very beginning of the essay writing process commences by researching your chosen topic. Read as much as you can about the topic from a variety of sources. Make a note of references so you can retrace your steps to vital sources. The use of the internet accelerates this process, especially if you use your university's library catalogue and the guided reading list. When using the internet do remember to only use reliable sources. Your ultimate goal is to become extremely knowledgeable in this subject. Sort the literature into sections such as recent research through to older research, countries of origin and theoretical strands. Whatever system you use to sort the literature, keep them organised.

2 *Analysis.* Following immersion within the literature, you will have a really good idea of the information available on the subject. Now is the time to start your analysis of this literature. Start analysing the arguments of the papers you are reading. Clearly define the claims, write out the reasons and the evidence. Look for weaknesses of logic and also strengths. Learning how to write an essay begins by learning how to analyse essays written by others.

3 *Mind map development.* The development of a mind map will help you organise your work following the analysis. Always draw the mind map in soft pencil, so that erasing will not leave distracting marks on the paper. Revisit the mind map many times. Take time away from it at regular intervals, so that each time you review it you see the contents clearly. Finally, you need to ensure that the mind map addresses the key requirements of the assessment.

4 *Outline.* Use headings (they may change with the development of your essay) to convey paragraphs or sections in your essay. Under the headings, use bullet points to indicate what contents will be included in each section. Map out the structure of your argument and make sure each paragraph is unified.

5 *Write the essay.* You have invested a large amount of time in your planning and it is now time to develop that outline further. Commence writing the paragraphs.

6 *Final step.* Proofread carefully, every line, every sentence. Check for spelling mistakes, ambiguity, referencing in the text and reference list (based on work of Johnson 2004).

Oral presentations/examinations

Now we're going to look at the development of an oral presentation and oral examination, as these are becoming a common assessment tool. They come in several forms: presentation of a poster, an oral examination or a time limited formal presentation. An oral exam may be used to assess your communication skills in medicine or during a medication round on the ward; to examine your knowledge of public health policies; to examine your counselling skills; or instruction of and delivery of art therapy to a client. One of the most important aspects to consider is the content of the work to be presented. Do not be fooled into thinking that you can 'blagg' your way through an oral exam. This type of exam needs just as much thorough preparation time and for you to acquire a considerable depth of knowledge and understanding of the subject as any other work. An oral exam relies on you knowing the necessary information and being able to recall it in exam conditions that really test your knowledge base.

Activity 7.1: Oral exam

List all the points that you consider to be important for an oral exam.

-
-
-
-
-
-
-
-

Preparation for an oral examination

Preparing for an oral examination will be similar to a written examination. However, the key to success is being able to verbalise the information in a coherent and logical manner – a difficult challenge when you are nervous. Very often the oral examination will focus on the learning outcomes of a module, project or research, so you will need to prepare around these themes. The use of prompt cards with key information (if allowed) will assist you in recalling the information during the oral examination, being a great source of support if your concentration lapses temporarily. You will be expected (depending on the academic level) to be able to discuss the information and cite key texts/authors/databases on the subject area.

Key tips for preparing for an oral exam

- Prepare the topic carefully and logically, just as you would for a written assignment.
- Be clear about what the objectives of the exam are (test of retained knowledge, test on depth of a specific topic, assessment of learning, validating the authenticity of your work).
- Write out a presentation in draft form. Review this and then prepare prompt cards which have key words, phrases, facts, data on them as aide-memoire for use in the exam. This should not be a complete script.
- Write out potential questions and appropriate responses.
- Practise, practise, then practise some more!
- Visualise yourself in the exam. What are you wearing? How are you sitting/standing?
- Visit the room where the exam is going to be held to desensitise you to the unfamiliarity of your surroundings.

The oral examination

It is important to set off in the right direction during an oral exam – the first few minutes really count, just as much as the last few minutes. Try and enter the room in a confident manner, without clutter or plastic bags rustling, or halfway through your lunchtime sandwich. Greet the examiners with a professional greeting: 'Good morning, ladies and gentlemen.' Tell the examiners who are you are and what you are about to present ('Hello, I am Jane, a third-year student nurse, and I am going to present . . .').

When you do commence the dialogue with the examiners, it is really important to speak in a clear, intelligible form and avoid the use of jargon, abbreviations, colloquialisms or words you struggle to pronounce. Remember, the examiner needs to understand you in order to mark your exam. Pay attention to the way you are sitting or standing as your body language is revealing. A hunched approach with no eye contact does not facilitate engagement, and can make an examiner feel distanced from your work. Conversely, appropriate eye contact and enthusiasm for your subject generates a far more pleasant interaction for you both.

Always keep to time. You are probably one of many students to be examined that day . When the examiner signals the end of your exam, do not be tempted to remain there for the next 20 minutes telling them everything you know or why you should pass. If you are using a power point presentation for your exam, never attempt to cram too much into the talk. It is better to précis the information on the slide and talk about the slide. Leave approximately two minutes per power point slide, or more if there are several points to be addressed. The examiners/audience will soon be bored by looking at the same slide for more than a few minutes. Do not be tempted to use animation for your amusement or to make up for lack of content. You may leave your examiners feeling rather irritated and distracted by the animation.

The dos and don'ts of oral examinations

Do

- Speak clearly and at an appropriate pace.
- Pause at all the key points to add a slight emphasis to them.
- Try and vary the pitch and tone of your voice to maintain the attention of the audience.
- Try and make eye contact with as many of the audience as possible to encourage them to engage with your presentation and to make examiners feel involved in what you are saying.
- Thank the audience for listening and invite questions.
- Consider asking a question to the audience at the end if no one else asks you anything.

Don't

- Digress away from your planned contents. You may either dig yourself a hole (metaphorically speaking), mention something you had not planned to mention, or lose your thread of the presentation.
- Avoid excessive gesticulations, excessive handwaving can be distracting.
- 'Eyeball' anyone or fix your eye contact on one person. It is embarrassing and inappropriate.

- Glare at everyone as if to say 'If you dare ask anything . . .'.
- Fidget and pace the floor.
- Stare at the overhead screen with your back to the audience.
- Make jokes – save them for outside the examination room.
- Read verbatim the context of slides – this is so boring to an examiner/audience.
- Read verbatim from a script. Again this is boring to an examiner/audience and you miss the opportunity to engage with them.
- Swear!

Key tips for the oral exam

- Appearance does matter. First impressions are formed very quickly. If you take your work seriously, chances are everyone else will too.
- Greet examiners appropriately.
- A depth of knowledge and good level of familiarity with your subject are crucial.
- Make appropriate eye contact with the examiners (do not glare at them even if they have just asked you the most horrendous question).
- Have prompt cards to hand in case of memory lapses – it can happen to us all!
- Keep to time.
- At the end, thank your audience for listening.
- After all your preparation you should be able to walk into the examination room with confidence.

Poster presentation

Now we're going to look at the development of a poster as these are produced in a different writing style from assignments. We will explore the designing of your poster and its presentation. Posters may be used to assess your knowledge of evidence-based research on a specific topic, to present a research study, demonstrate how a piece of equipment works, to clarify a process or to assess your knowledge of medical procedure. Whatever the purpose of the poster, its key use is to pass on information to the reader. Therefore, when designing your poster it is essential that the visual appearance and contents are equally considered. There is a finite amount of space available on a poster, so it will be necessary to condense the relevant information into small sections in a specific format. Detailed planning before submission is therefore crucial to ensure that you capture all the relevant information in the poster to meet the assessment criteria, and to omit any unnecessary information.

Activity 7.2 Poster

Think about a poster that you found visually appealing. You may have seen it on a bus, at a train station, on a board in the university, in the library.

Identify the key features that attracted you to read this poster:

-
-
-
-
-
-

It is important that the information on a poster is clear, presented in a logical order, legible and attractively presented. To guide you on some of these key points consider the following:

- Poster presentations come in all shapes and sizes. However, the size of a poster may be governed by the audience who will be viewing it. A conference poster usually has to be of a specific dimension. For submission as a university assessment, the assessment brief will dictate the size of poster required.
- The number of sections of the poster will vary according to the poster's function. So, for example, if the poster is to share the findings of a research study, the sections might include a background, introduction, methodology, findings, discussion, conclusion and references. Therefore each section requires equal attention to detail.
- Think of the poster as a circular process, where each section is read and considered in conjunction with the preceding and subsequent sections. This will ensure the poster has a logical and coherent flow of information.

- Try and find a graphic for the poster that symbolises the topic (ensure it is not copyrighted).
- Use clear headings that stand out.
- Be cautious in the use of colour. Strips are very dazzling to the examiner.
- Use a font size big enough to ensure the examiner isn't using a magnifying glass to read it! If the poster is being presented at a conference, it may be read from a viewing distance of up to two metres. Therefore, it is essential that the font size is adequate and the text legible.
- Avoid the temptation to cram in so much information that each section is dense with text. This is really offputting to anyone who dares venture near to read it.

Designing your poster

There are two approaches that can be used to design a poster.

Approach 1

The poster is designed as one complete document (see Figure 7.1). The design of the poster can be altered, such as background colour, dimensions, headings, by using computer software. The poster can be designed in any size, and therefore the student can see the whole poster on the computer screen. Producing one-piece posters can take patience as you get used to the process. Therefore, ensure you start work on it in plenty of time before the submission date. When you print the poster, it can be enlarged to the size required. Caution is required if you have uploaded photographs as their clarity photos on enlargement is dependent upon the number of pixels. The fewer pixels used, the poorer the clarity of the photo when enlarged.

Approach 2

This method of poster design uses a different power point slide for each section of the poster (see Figure 7.2). All these slides are then put together to become the completed poster. As in Approach 1, the poster can be designed in any size, but the student can usually only see one section of the poster on the computer screen at a time. However, when you print the poster, it can be formatted to merge as one poster and also enlarged to the size required.

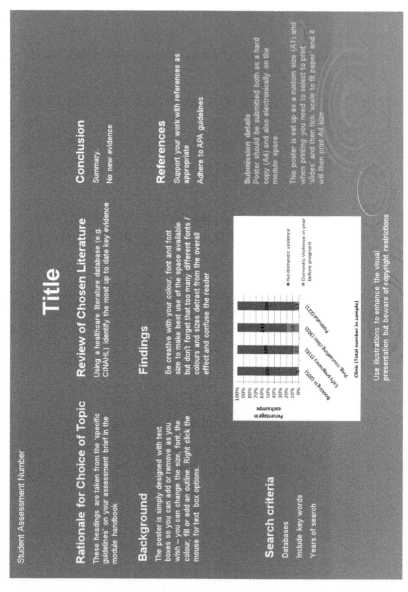

Figure 7.1 Example of a poster using Approach 1

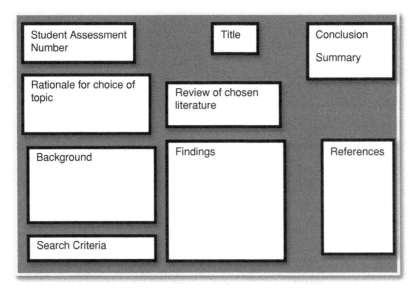

Figure 7.2 Example of a poster using Approach 2

Poster format

To enable the reader to understand the contents of the poster, it is important that the contents follow a logical sequence. The use of headings will clarify each section of the poster and assist the reader in navigating through the poster in the logical sequence. Consider the poster as a circular piece of work, in which each section does not 'sit' in isolation, but rather each section of the poster is related and affects the sections before and after (see Figure 7.1). The conclusion section summarises the contents of the poster, drawing conclusions from the evidence that has been presented.

Presenting the poster

Preparing to present your poster for assessment or at a conference is very similar to preparing for an examination. You will be expected to be able to converse with the examiner or conference delegates, demonstrating a good depth of knowledge of all information presented in the poster, to be able to answer questions on the topic, expand on key points and engage in academic debate. The use of prompt cards might help alleviate nerves and producing handouts will enable you to provide the individuals with further information.

Figure 7.3 Thought process for developing your own poster

Key tips for poster presentation.

- Prepare prompt cards around the key themes of your poster.
- Practise answering questions.
- Ensure that you understand everything on your poster (i.e. you can define all words/terminology used).
- Ensure the poster is visually appealing and that the examiner/ audience can read it.
- Make sure that you do not have too much information on the poster as people will lose interest.
- Make eye contact with potential readers and smile! People won't want to stop and read it if you glare at them.

Time limited formal presentation

Submitting and presenting a poster under a time constraint requires the student to have an excellent depth of knowledge of the content of the poster, to be able to recall all the key points presented and to verbalise these to the audience. To simply read verbatim the contents of the poster is very monotonous and not good practice. All examiners have the ability to read it for themselves. Consider the use of prompt cards and rehearse your presentation very well in order to give a really good performance.

When presenting your poster there are some elements that are more important to focus on than others. You do not need to discuss the overall design, colour scheme, size of text or poster structure. For example, in presenting a poster that demonstrates the findings of a research study, some attention must be paid to the background of the study and existing literature, but the main thrust of the presentation should be shared between the methodology, the findings and the relevance of the findings in the discussion section. For a poster presentation of evidence based practice, the focus would be on what research studies the evidence has originated from, what it has demonstrated and how that has been applied to practice.

Key tips

- Do not read verbatim from the presentation.
- Use notes pages to help script the presentation but make sure these are key points rather than a full script.
- Face the audience not the screen.
- Do not use too many fancy animations/sounds/cartoons as these detract from the points you are trying to make.
- Use terms that you can pronounce as any difficult words will trip you up and disrupt the flow.
- Time the presentation to ensure you adhere to the time limits and practise using the equipment so you know how to open the presentation, put it on to slideshow and operate the slides.
- Do not have too much information on the slides.
- Select a professional looking background that complements the topic.
- Ensure that you address all elements of the brief.
- Ensure that you use references on the slides and have a reference list as a final slide.
- Prepare for questions.

Dissertation

A popular method of assessment as part of the final year of an under-graduate course is assessment by dissertation. A dissertation can at first seem a daunting task as it is often the largest single piece of work that is submitted as part of a degree programme. Therefore, this section intends to help you structure your work and makes suggestions on how to overcome the initial and long-term anxieties many students face when completing a substantial piece of work. There are two areas to consider in a dissertation: how you feel towards developing a dissertation and how to write a dissertation. This section of the chapter addresses both these aspects. As the old adage goes: 'Fail to plan and you plan to fail'.

Be clear about the task

The word dissertation has different meanings, so your first task is to establish what you actually have to do. For example, are you required to carry out empirical research or is it a research proposal where no actual research occurs?

Planning the dissertation

The first key principle when planning and writing a dissertation is to establish a timeline. This may seem obvious but every dissertation student who has been through this process will tell you that time 'slips through your fingers' and things always take longer than expected. So let's work on an academic year of 12 months and plan the work, presuming that the work will be submitted in month 12. The principle of this plan can be adapted to a shorter timeline and is intended to be an illustrative example only.

The development of the writing of each section of your dissertation will now be discussed.

Structuring and writing the dissertation

Regardless of which approach you are expected to follow, there are some standard principles that will be expected. Here we are going to concentrate on the structure of a dissertation when empirical research is used. We identify the structure of the dissertation and provide you, the reader, with pointers on how to write each section

Table 7.1 Example timeline for a dissertation

Month	Task
1	Formation of ideas. Initial literature search. Initial meeting with supervisor to discuss ideas and plans.
2	Extensive literature review. First draft of literature review chapter.
3	Submission of first draft (introduction and literature review). Development of methodological approach. Completion of ethics forms.
4	Writing of the research proposal. Writing of methodology chapter. Submission to ethics committee.
5	Recruitment of sample. Submission of draft methodology chapter for review by supervisor.
6	Data collection and continued writing.
7	Data collection and continued writing.
8	Data analysis.
9	Writing of results chapter and submission of draft.
10	Writing of the discussion chapter and recommendations.
11	Submission of final draft to supervisor. Final proofread. Binding of dissertation.
12	Submission of dissertation.

Title page

This should be written clearly with careful attention to spelling and grammar. This is the first page of your dissertation so it needs to impress the examiner. Do not be tempted to put too much information on this page. Usually the title page contains important information only, your name and/or student number, the title of the dissertation and your supervisor (if required).

Index

This is the next page and should list of all the component parts of the dissertation with a page number for each section.

Abstract

This section should be the last section of the dissertation to be written because it is a synopsis (overview) of the whole of the research project. The following aspects should be included in the abstract: background, literature, methodology, results, discussion and recommendations. To write an abstract, try writing it a line at a time. First, read the background section of your dissertation and then write two sentences that summarise it. Then read the literature review and write two sentences that summarise what is already known about your study. Use your own words to prevent plagiarism here as it is not appropriate to use references in an abstract. Read the methodology section and write two sentences that include all the main points of this section such as ethical approval, sample size, consent, data collection tool, method of analysis. Read your findings section and condense this into two sentences. Finally, write two sentences to summarise the findings. Write one sentence on the importance and then recommendations of this study. After all this, you should re-read and refine your abstract. A helpful hint here is to look at abstracts in peer reviewed journals.

Chapter 1 Introduction and background

This section, as a general rule, should be no longer than two or three pages, although this will vary according the specific guidelines given. Here you should clearly outline the background to the research study: for example, if your research question was examining clients' coping strategies following a form of cancer, you would define the cancer, discuss the incidence, highlight why this area needs further investigation, this could be from your practical experience and observations. At the end of this section you should outline the layout of the subsequent chapters.

Chapter 2 Literature review

This section provides the evidence and rationale for the study. First, you need to provide a detailed summary of how you obtained the literature. So here you will be expected to state which databases you accessed (for example, medline, CINAHL), the key words you used and the number of research papers found, how you filtered these and finally the number used in this section to present a critical discussion. Once the literature search is complete, the format of this chapter should be a discussion of the research papers in themes, rather than a critical discussion of each research paper individually. The use of theme subheadings would structure the development of the discussion. To write a literature review section of the dissertation, it is necessary to present an argument that addresses your research question, by discussing existing research in the field, identifying potential limitations, and identifying why your chosen method of study is relevant. To achieve this level of critical analysis (see Chapter 4) the research articles need to be read thoroughly and understood.

Further reading

- *Doing a Literature Review in Health and Social Care: A Practical Guide*, by Helen Aveyard (2010) Maidenhead: Open University Press.
- *Succeeding with your Literature Review: A Handbook for Students*, by Paul Oliver (2012) Maidenhead: Open University Press.

Chapter 3 Research question and aims

At the end of the literature review chapter, the research question should be detailed with the research aims. This then leads on to the methodology chapter. The methodology chapter is usually subdivided into smaller sections including: methodology, ethical consideration, sample and access to sample, data collection tool, method of analysis.

Methodology

This section should start broadly and funnel down to the specific methods you have adopted. You need to define your theoretical perspective, and introduce the paradigm to be used. You then need to write about your methodology. Writing this section is factual and referenced throughout. It is important in this section that you write it clearly and ensure that the reader can see you understand the methodology you have chosen to use, and that it is the most appropriate for your research project. Also within this section you will need to clearly outline an understanding of sampling and sample selection, again discussing pros and cons. Data collection also needs to be clearly discussed and ethics.

Further reading

- *Research Methods in Health: Investigating Health and Health Services*, by Ann Bowling (2009) Maidenhead: Open University Press.

Chapter 4 Results

This section is written in a factual precise way, ensuring there is no ambiguity of results. Write a detailed discussion on the analysis of the data, including, for example, the number recruited to the study and the number of questionnaires returned. A simple table would be useful illustrating the sample, age, gender and number. In addition you will be required to highlight the process of data analysis: for instance, whether you have used a statistical package, or for qualitative data what frameworks you have used, for example, a form of thematic analysis. The use of tables, graphs and diagrams would be useful to illustrate quantitative data, whereas quotes from the semi structured interviews are expected when using qualitative data. Whatever the data you should present it in a logical format, with the use of subheadings or themes to structure the presentation of results.

Chapter 5 Discussion

Your discussion section should be written in a style that presents the factual information of your data, whilst drawing on the literature presented in Chapter 2, the literature review section. You need to write about what your findings mean in the context of existing literature, and identify whether your findings are the same as in the literature, or whether they reveal something different. Be careful here not to 'hype up' your findings, being too ambitious about what they reveal. This is a common mistake. Keep the focus of the discussion section on the important points of the findings. The discussion section usually also contains a small subsection of *Recommendations* of the research project. The use of bullet points clarifies this section.

References

This section should conform to the preferred university reference system. Time should be taken to record all references used in a logical format and we would recommend that you use an electronic referencing system. A final check before submission should occur of all references used throughout the text against the reference list ensuring there are no incorrect or absent entries.

Appendices

These need to be relevant and appropriate. The participant information sheet, consent form, questionnaire (if used), semi-structured interview questions (if used) and ethical approval should all be included.

Further reading

- *Doing Your Research Project: A Guide for First-Time Researchers in Education, Health and Social Care*, by Judith Bell (2010) Maidenhead: Open University Press.
- *The Social Work Dissertation: Using Small – Scale Qualitative Methodology*, by Malcolm Carey (2013) Maidenhead: Open University Press.
- *Excellent Dissertations!*, by Peter Levin (2011) Maidenhead: Open University Press.

Activity 7.3 Dissertation action plan

Now you have read this section of the chapter, consider your individual action plan to develop your dissertation.

-
-
-
-
-
-
-
-

Portfolio development

Now we are going to look at the development of a portfolio as most professional bodies require the development of a professional portfolio that remains contemporaneous throughout your career. The aim of a portfolio is to demonstrate that you have met and continue to meet the professional requirements of your governing body. A portfolio has become an essential component of most professional programmes and is used to record all your professional training courses, qualifications and work experience. Think of your portfolio as a 'living document' and one that needs updating each year.

The most important aspect of a portfolio is that it is a 'show and tell' of your ability to perform a specific job. For example, if you are applying for a specialised job, then your portfolio should demonstrate to your future employers that you can fulfil this role. Small details make a difference. You want to be taken seriously when you apply for a job so make sure your portfolio looks the part – clean folder, clearly labelled, each section separated, being consistent in the style of headings, font and font size.

The portfolio is usually required to present evidence of learning in a concise manner, using reflection (see Chapter 5) to identify areas of learning and development over a period of time. Issues of confidentiality need careful consideration to avoid identification of staff, patients or work areas. The construction of each entry will depend on the specific guidelines set out. The headings listed here provide an overview of some of the things you may need to consider.

Construction and writing a portfolio

Title page

Type your name and insert a small appropriate photograph of yourself.

Table of contents

Clearly identify the contents of your portfolio.

Personal statement

This is a crucial part of your portfolio and needs to impress any reader. This statement defines who you are, what you are capable of and how you function in respect of your chosen profession in health and social care. As such, it needs to be written in an articulate and logical manner. Construct your personal statement as you would an essay (see earlier section of this chapter) to ensure a structured approach to your writing.

Curriculum vitae

Most portfolios should start with a curriculum vitae (CV). This will include information on you, your education, current and past employment. Write your CV in a factual way, making all the information very clear to a reader (see Table 7.2).

Table 7.2 Headings for a CV

Personal details

Insert small professional photograph of yourself

Full name:

Address:

Contact tel number (home):

(mobile):

E-mail address: absmith@email.com

Driving licence – e.g. clean UK driving licence

Professional qualifications

Most recent first and include date of award (e.g.):

2013 NVQ Level 3 Health Care, College of Technology, Liverpool

2010 NVQ Level 2 Health Care, College of Technology, Liverpool

Employment history

Most recent job first. List dates of employment, post held, department and site.

Do not leave blanks in employment history if at all possible (people are suspicious of blanks in employment history).

Current roles and responsibilities

Awards

Referees. Prospective employers will want to contact your previous manager to ask about you.

Hobbies and interests. Do not ramble on, write this section in clear and concise terms.

Assessments

The next section of your portfolio is then dependent on your profession and guidance will be given by your programme lecturers. Generally this section should follow a basic format:

- Practice assessments/placement reports, including records of achievement, clinical assessment documents, skills inventories and learning logs.

- Theoretical assessments, including examples of work and assignment feedback sheets.

Both of these assessments should have been written by your mentors and are photocopies of the original documents.

Personal reflections

This section would include evidence of inter-professional learning/ working, critical incidents and reflections on practice. There will be professional requirements that have to be met in this section and it needs to be written at an appropriate academic level for your job (see Chapter 4 for level of writing). Write these using a reflective model (see Chapter 5), and ensure they are referenced throughout with an appropriate level of critical analysis (see Chapter 4). Emphasise your personal learning as this is a powerful tool when attending job interviews, as you can then clearly demonstrate that you are a progressive and responsive learner that responds to incidents. Provide a summary at the end of each reflection identifying your own learning from each.

Evidence of achieving professional standards

This section would be completed once you have achieved your professional qualification. For further information please access your professional body websites and written guidance, and your programme learning outcomes. However, this section would usually incorporate a photocopy of all your certificates and qualifications, including any training programmes/courses you have attended or additional learning undertaken.

Additional information

This would include details of any student bodies you have joined or if you have represented the university at an event, plus any letters of thanks from individuals which are relevant to your professional qualification.

Key tips for writing portfolios

- Consider them a textual replica of who you are – make them accurate and professional.
- Write them clearly and in an articulate way.

- Clearly signpost each section of your portfolio, making it easy for a reader to navigate their way through it.
- Always be honest throughout.
- Clearly identify your learning through reflection.
- Keep your portfolio file clean and smoke free.
- Always use photocopies of original documents/certificates, never use originals.
- Maintain anonymity and confidentiality at all times. Block out any identifiable information on clinical records, mentor assessor reports, ward names, etc.

Writing for publication

The final part of this chapter will explore writing for publication. All students should consider the merit of publishing their work. This is particularly pertinent to those whose work is awarded a high mark. However, all students should have this opportunity and consider publishing their work, as it is a great motivator to improve your standard of work and a great experience to see your work in print.

Many universities have their own inhouse journal specifically for this purpose. Usually the student accesses support from the member of academic staff who guided their work prior to submission, to enable the student to transform the assignment into a paper for publication. It then becomes a joint venture between the student and supervisor. A journal is only one of many places where a student can publish work. Consider writing a short article for a newsletter, a church magazine or a newspaper. All these provide excellent experience for writing for other people.

Aims of publishing

- To see your hard work in print.
- To share your research findings, opinions and excellent pieces of work.
- To encourage academic debate.
- To encourage interest in your publication.
- To promote your opportunity of employment, promotion, development of your career.

Key tips for publishing your work

- Enjoy working with a published member of staff who will help your professional development in writing for publication.
- Choose the journal for submission of your article carefully. Read the journal's aims and ensure your article matches these.
- Adhere to all of the Journal's guidelines for the format of your article (referencing style, length of article, length of abstract, headings to be used, etc.).
- Proofread your work carefully to ensure excellent grammar, syntax and punctuation.
- If at first you don't succeed, reformat the article and try again in another journal.

Conclusion

Assessment of work within higher education can be achieved through many different media. This chapter has sought to identify and illuminate the nuances between these formats. It has provided activities for students to complete and highlighted the key points for each format. Although each format has a specific purpose and may assess students' work in a different way, such as an oral exam compared to a written essay, there is a commonality between them. That is, each format of assessment requires thorough planning, adherence to the assessment briefs and writing at the required academic level. There is no substitute for these things. To be successful in academic work you must also seek advice, guidance and support when needed and be proactive in recognising your learning needs and challenges.

Hints and tips

Each format of assessment provides you the student with an opportunity to demonstrate your knowledge base and skills. A common feature of all assessments is the amount of time required to obtain a good mark. Time therefore needs to be set aside to format, edit and revise your work before submission. We also recommend the following advice:

- Always start your work in plenty of time (think how long it may take you and then double it!).
- Plan and develop study timetables.
- Seek advice and guidance if you are unsure.
- Access the support on offer, for example, student development weeks, tutorials and learning seminars.
- Adhere to the referencing system of the institution.
- Revisit the assessment guidelines to ensure you have addressed all the key point and requirements.

Reference

Johnson, T. (2004) *Ten Steps to Writing an Essay*. The American School in Cairo. http://www1.aucegypt.edu/academic/writers/research.htm.

8

Students' experiences of writing

Richard Williams, Michael Baksh, Dasha Koneva, Mary Williams and James Greaves

---

This chapter explores the different perspectives of five health and social care students on the following topics:

- Personal motivations for writing
- Initial feelings towards academic writing
- Finding out what to expect from writing
- Learning how to write well in health and social care
- Advice for other students

Introduction

This chapter focuses on the students' unique perspective on writing, as told in their own words. Five students, from a broad range of backgrounds, ages and learning requirements have contributed to this chapter. They share personal experiences of writing whilst studying within health and social care.

The chapter presents excerpts from their stories that focus on their journey of acquisition of writing skills in higher education. Interspersed within this chapter are also activities for you to engage with. There is signposting to specific sections of the previous chapters to enable you to revisit essential texts and plan your own development.

It is important to remember that the excerpts in this chapter are from students who are currently studying, or have recently graduated from, a programme of study within health and social care. We would like to thank them for sharing their experiences and feelings, and hope that their journeys will inspire you, the reader. Our thanks go to Richard Williams, Michael Baksh, Dasha Koneva, Mary Williams and James Greaves.

Student profiles

Richard Williams is 25, and a recent graduate of a North West University where he successfully gained a Diploma in Higher Education with Nursing and Midwifery (NMC) Registration as a Mental Health Nurse.

Michael Baksh is a 43 year old 'mature student' and has recently been awarded a BSc (Hons) degree in Pre-registration Nursing. Prior to commencing his university programme of study, he spent 14 years working in financial services.

Dasha Koneva 35, graduated with a BSc (Hons) degree in Pre-registration Nursing in 2010. Dasha came to the UK from Russia. English is not her first language.

Mary Williams is studying medicine at a Russell Group rated university. Her journey to university was not easy as she initially started an economics degree at a different university. It became immediately evident to her that she had made the wrong choice of career. Some months later she decided to research her options for studying medicine. Although she had the right A-level grades they were in the wrong subjects, resulting in her having to find a course that would prepare her adequately for applying to study medicine at university.

James Greaves is 21 years old and has recently been awarded a BSc (Hons) degree in Pre-registration Nursing. James was diagnosed with dyslexia, dyspraxia and Irlens syndrome at the beginning of his university programme of study.

Personal motivations for writing

We each have individual motivational reasons for writing. Indeed, our motivations came from a variety of sources. It is often through a process of reflection that we understand what these individual motivations are, and how they impact on us. Chapter 5 introduces the reader to a variety of models of reflection, and it is through this process of reflection that our thoughts can become clear. It is important to question ourselves to define where our motivation has originated from, as this can serve to boost our confidence and determination to seek help and support to enable us to fulfil our ambitions in writing.

> As a result of my personal circumstances I had a big change in my life, the country, the language and career. Although I had had some experience in academic writing, it was all very long ago, I needed to start from scratch. English is not my first language and academic or even any writing is not the easiest task for me. My first experience of writing in the university has presented me with a challenge. First of all, everything I have written in English before was for my English studies; therefore, I had been concentrating on the language rather than content. Now, at the university, I needed to produce not only a grammatically correct written piece but also meaningful and within the advised structure and size.
>
> (Darena)

> I was unprepared for the intensity of this one year course and was very naive when it came to academic writing. My only previous experience of academic writing was during my A levels which, with the benefit of hindsight, I now realise was nothing remotely of an adequate standard for university level writing. I was starting from a very basic level.
>
> (Mary)

> My education has been blighted by disinterest and laziness throughout my formative years! I left school at 16 years of age with GCSEs all at D grade or lower. However, my interest in academic studies emerged when with a friend, we began mental health nursing. Although I would say writing at university (or at any time) does not come easily to me, I have come to realise that it is crucial and important at a number of levels. Not only was I able to make a success of my studies, but writing at university, in the form of written assignments, proved to be excellent preparation for writing reports in my first qualified nurse job.
>
> (Richard)

> I had spent the last 14 years of my life working as a financial planning manager, advising clients on life assurance, pensions, savings

and investments, and prior to that for a firm of solicitors as an accounts clerk and court clerk. I knew I wanted to work in nursing by this stage, and was very excited and proud to be accepted on to this degree course.

(Mike)

I knew that I wanted a career in nursing and I was determined to give the BSc degree my best shot and full attention. My motivation towards my work included remembering why I chose nursing as a career. The small things would keep me motivated such as seeing the university emblem on a colleague's uniform, witnessing fellow students leave the course, and hearing kind words on completing my work.

(James)

Activity 8.1 Personal motivations

List your personal motivations for writing well in health and social care:

1
2
3
4
5
6
7
8
9
10

Initial feelings towards academic writing

The students' comments reflect the diversity of their backgrounds and pre-higher education experiences. These excerpts bring together feelings that may be experienced by many other students when commencing their programme of study. The majority of programmes within health and social care involve the student spending a proportion of their time learning within the university, and also in practice. This places extra demand upon students. As such, it is beneficial for students to reflect (see Chapter 5) on their current feelings toward academic writing, in order to identify where they need to progress to, in order to succeed.

> It would be fair to say that I had no idea what academic writing was. My previous experiences had not prepared me in any way and I developed a high level of anxiety about all that it entailed. I didn't even feel comfortable in how, and what, I should be reading. I had no experience of referencing adequately, very little knowledge of library databases or how to access and use the catalogue. I even struggled to fully understand the assessment brief provided by my module leaders. I needed much more detail than that which was provided and I agonised over potentially misinterpreting what was required of me. I simply did not know where or how to start reading, let alone writing.
>
> (Richard)

> I felt that as a nurse I needed to develop a language that would be understandable for a wide range of people without using simplistic words or on the contrary academic jargon. Additionally, from very early in my nursing studies I realised that I would like to be involved in research as a research nurse and nurse researcher. Both of those roles imply ability to write at appropriate academic level therefore this skill needed to become second nature for me.
>
> (Dasha)

> The specific challenges of writing at medical school include learning from other written work, e.g. tutor prepared guidance notes, reading for writing purposes, referencing techniques. At first I found the jargon overpowering and the Vancouver referencing technique a little alien so I took time to get to grips with this.
>
> (Mary)

> I have found academic writing in higher education challenging because of the 22 years that had elapsed since I was last in education. I feel that being a mature student has advantages over some of the younger students, especially on a vocational course such as this [Adult Nursing]. The benefits of life experience cannot be underestimated; those personal and professional interactions that I have experienced throughout my working life, have enabled me to transfer key skills to this new learning challenge.
>
> (Mike)

At first I was not too nervous when I started university, as I did not think that was a big jump from college to university. However, when discussing the three years of assignments and lectures regarding the levels of academic writing, the nerves soon kicked in. I was looking through power points on guidance towards academic writing and, in the back of my head, I started to doubt that I would be able to write to the level that was expected of me. I voiced my concerns to my tutor. I also accessed learning support services and after an assessment I was diagnosed with dyslexia, dyspraxia and Irlens syndrome. An educational psychologist identified the appropriate support that would help me in my university studies.

(James)

Activity 8.2 Concerns about academic writing

Think about any concerns you might have towards academic writing. Write these down in the left-hand column.

Concerns towards academic writing	How to resolve the issue
1	
2	
3	
4	
5	

Now revisit your list and using the chapters in this book think of ways of resolving these issues. Identify these in the right-hand column.

Finding out what to expect from writing

New students to heath and social care might feel overwhelmed when they commence their programme of study, with all the new information provided for them, as well as perhaps settling into

new surroundings. Managing all this information may be challenging and requires the student to develop keen organisational skills
from the earliest opportunity. This organisational requirement also
impacts on their reading and writing towards various assignments.
Developing strategies to help organise their own work is useful.

> I approached writing in all the wrong ways. I left everything to the
> last minute and often left myself with little or no time to seek sup-
> port and guidance from my tutors, despite this being on offer. Writ-
> ing is not something I like doing or comes naturally to me. I found
> the prospect of writing assignments on a topic completely new to
> me very daunting. My advice to anyone writing at university is to
> avoid putting yourself in such a position, as the level of stress I put
> myself through was completely avoidable. In my experience I found
> reading became much easier once I became more familiar with the
> subject. As I became more self-aware I was increasingly more moti-
> vated to read around the topic so in this way I could ensure that the
> required reading was done.
>
> (Richard)

> I soon learned that university level study significantly differs from
> any previous experiences I had had and for those of you reading
> this who are of the view that you will be 'spoon-fed' to the same
> level you were at school or college, think again! Halfway through
> my first year at university I was asked to answer a predetermined
> essay question and conduct a literature review based on that title.
> At this point I had very little understanding of what a literature
> review was, never mind carrying one out. I was unprepared for
> the task and a little shocked to realise how little guidance I would
> be given. I literally didn't know where to begin. Before I could even
> contemplate starting the review I had to get to grips with the library
> catalogue and database system, as well as other online resources
> and finding relevant journals. Most universities will offer a library
> induction and tutorial which tends to take just over an hour and
> provides a run-through of all the basics you will need. Regretfully,
> I didn't attend my tutorial.
>
> Once I started to search for literature I realised I would have ben-
> efited from more guidance but as too much time had lapsed before
> realising this I learned, with the benefit of hindsight, to regret the
> decision not to learn about the library resources. I do not hesitate
> therefore to advise all students to attend these tutorials and spend a
> day searching around the databases and reading different journals.

In addition, I have realised that in everyday reading, if you happen across something related to your work then save it to your computer; you never know when it will be useful.

(Mary)

Regardless of whether I had a learning difficulty or not, my personal academic tutor was able to signpost the support available and refer me to different support departments within the campus to ensure I received the correct help, whether it was for my emotional, physical or intellectual health. I was lucky to have such a supporting and understanding personal academic tutor who pushed me to know my limits and strengths and to use them both to my advantage. All of the module lecturers had always got time to sit down and ensure that I understood what to expect in forthcoming assignments. The great thing about the university as a whole was the ability to plan assignments and have them approved, ensuring that I was on the right tracks before I wrote 3000 words of incorrect and unnecessary work.

(James)

It took me a while to develop a good approach to writing. My first point of contact was a tutor who set the assignment. My tutors helped me to understand the aim of the assignments and provided references for extra reading. With their help I have achieved a greater understanding of the subject and developed my writing style. Initially I have struggled with structuring the essay. One of my tutors has recommended me to seek advice of the learning support. They were great and the help they provided was invaluable. In addition to reading my drafts and correcting some spelling errors, I was recommended a few books on essay planning and structuring, as well as books about how to manage my time and learning. I know that many people, including me, find referencing quite challenging. The learning support and librarians helped me with my problems. I also learned that librarians are the best people to ask about the use of online services, libraries and other electronic resources. It felt like everybody at the university was there for you to succeed.

(Dasha)

At the beginning of each academic year I have made it a priority to attend a workshop held by the university's learning support services in order to understand what the minimum standards are for the level of writing which was required for the assignments that year. I found this to be an invaluable exercise which helped me progress my learning, as it identified and explained the key words and terms used in the assessment briefs. My second port of call was the library, where the highly knowledgeable and helpful staff were available to teach me how to use the assortment of databases required to research my subjects.

(Mike)

Activity 8.3 Support available

List all the support that is available for you to access, to support you in writing in health and social care. By each one, identify which day and date you will access this support. We have started this list for you.

University's learning support services	Date: Day: Contact number: E-mail:
Personal academic tutor	Date: Day: Contact number: E-mail:

Learning how to write well in health and social care

When we enter a new environment such as higher education, or indeed when we start learning a new sport or hobby, there is a specific set of skills that accompanies that environment. Within higher education, one of the new skills is academic writing. It is a skill that we have to develop, work at and craft, and once learnt we can forge onwards to develop it further. Mary, James, Richard, Mike and

Dasha have shared with us their experiences of how they developed their skills to write well in health and social care. They talk of the techniques that they have developed or been supported to develop, and how this has positively impacted their writing.

> My writing usually started with mapping out the key aspects of the assignment, my 'spider' map. It consisted of the main working title of the assignment with a number of thought bubbles containing key themes surrounding it. I then used these themes to construct my main body of writing. I discovered that the best way for me to write was to put down all the information I had including my thoughts and even some random observations or conclusions I was drawing together from the literature. I was then able to construct a coherent essay by editing what I had written to make sure I complied with the allocated word count. I tackled the introduction and conclusion last of all as I was more familiar with the topic at the end and could draw together all the ideas I had written about.
>
> Last of all I checked it over for spelling and grammar and asked a critical friend to read through it. Most students I have met spend huge amounts of time worrying about how to reference or worse still concluding that referencing is not important. I very nearly fell into this trap. Although I found referencing a real 'pain' at first, I learned very quickly to take notice of how to reference properly. I did not feel comfortable or confident with referencing until I was introduced to a piece of computer software (EndNote). This was immediately beneficial and removed all anxiety related to referencing.
>
> (Richard)

> For me, preparing to write an academic assignment began with spending valuable time understanding what is required, doing some initial background reading about the topic and attempting to find some historical information to put it all into context. The next stage of preparation involved searching for relevant literature material and reading all the academic papers I found. I found particularly useful highlighting key bits of information in every literature source I used. This was important to me as I need things to be laid out in front of me in a logical order. To clearly set this out I developed a table matrix where I wrote down each of the journal titles, publication dates and summarised the paper including methodologies used, key statistics, findings or other relevant information to see all the key information in front of me. I was then able to begin to see that some were more useful than others.

Once I had selected the literature to be used I was able to identify key themes running throughout them all. It was these themes that eventually enabled me to organise my writing and ensured that it read well and had a logical order. I found that the best way to organise the main body of my written assignment was to use sub-headings, and for my literature review I used themes to separate out the text. This proved to be useful in giving my writing some structure instead of trying to get everything down at once. I found this uniquely helpful as I was able to concentrate on one aspect of my writing at a time. I was advised to use a reputable reference manager system so before starting to write my assignments I was already inputting all the academic literature sources I came across, even the ones I eventually didn't use. This built up my personal library very quickly.

(Mary)

Before I start writing anything I needed to understand aspects of the topic that were particularly important and needed be included and what could be left out. In order to do this, I read the assessment brief a few times and talked to different people about the topic to get a different perspective on it. This helped me to consolidate my thoughts and develop my own ideas. It was often not what they [peers] told me that mattered but the discussion itself. I then wrote down some ideas and started reading.

In my opinion successful academic essays depend on the amount of reading that has been done before the start of writing. Reading provided me with knowledge and deeper understanding of the topic I was writing about, extended my vocabulary and helped to develop my writing style. I tried to read a wide range of literature: textbooks, news articles, papers in scientific journals, etc; following up the references and citations for the material I had read. I kept all the references of the papers I had read in preparation for writing, even if they did not seem relevant. The more I learnt about the subject the easier it was to write.

Whilst I was in the reading stage of the preparation I start developing a plan of the piece. The plan was a skeleton of my essay and helped me to stay focused on the topic. I also planned the amount I needed to write on each point in the plan. I started writing the main body of my essay from the part I felt most comfortable about. It gave me a sort of a push and made it easier to start writing about other things in the essays. I wrote sentences and paragraphs, read them and rewrote them again. Sometimes this process seemed to have no end, but eventually it finished either with the best possible result or more often with the deadline.

Usually I asked people to read confusing bits of the assignment in order to help me understand what I meant. I am very lucky as my family were always happy to read and criticise my writing. I think it was always beneficial to have an opinion of an independent person on my work. I could clarify anything that needed further explaining and get rid of the repetitions. When my essay was more or less finished, it was time to show it to a person who actually understood what I am writing about (a tutor). The tutor feedback on the draft was an important tool in moulding the piece to the brief.

(Dasha)

As with life's problems, I tend to look at things from a logical perspective, breaking things down into smaller steps that will follow sequentially and will allow my writing to progress smoothly from one step or point to the next. I find this highly beneficial as it ensures I do not miss anything out. The assessment brief, provided by the university, will have a series of learning objectives, a guide for the content of the assignment. Once I knew what topic my assignment was on, it was time to access the library databases, and do some reading around my chosen topic. The next stage in writing my assignment was planning, and having that structure to work to helped me focus my ideas.

(Mike)

Learning how to write within the health and social care faculty was challenging but again support was available in the sense of support tutors who were aware of our expectation within the faculty and clear written assignment briefs that were made available to us. Each module had specific reading lists and useful links to health care based databases which would allow us to search the information required for that assignment. Subject librarians were always on hand to help us search for the best information.

I would say that mind mapping made it easier when planning my assignments. Loads of student preferred to write their notes and draw their plans. However, I am much more focused when it comes to assignments. I preferred my home environment when planning or taking my laptop to tutorials with me. During tutorials I used certain gadgets to ensure that I would understand my notes when reading them later on at home as I had tendencies to write a lot of notes but forget why I wrote them. The best decision I made was to ensure that I understood what was required in the assignment by referring to the module learning outcomes, and also the assessment brief.

(James)

Activity 8.4 Developing writing skills

Draw a mind map/bubble diagram/thought chart to identify how you will develop your skill in writing in higher education.

How I will learn to write in health and social care

Advice for other students

Learning by doing is an established way of approaching the acquisition of any new skill, including writing well in health and social care. All the students who have contributed to this chapter have learnt in this way, developing their craft of academic writing over a period of three years or more, and each one successfully graduating from their chosen programme of study.

College and university is for adult learners so don't expect to have the work done for you as it is your responsibility and if you want the qualification that much you will achieve your goal.

(James)

Go to any tutorials that are offered. These may seem tedious at first but you will use the information they give you sooner rather than later.

(Mary)

Avoid putting yourself in an impossible position through protracted procrastination. Adopt strategies to begin writing something down on paper. This reduces stress levels and writing-related stress is avoidable. Reading will become much easier once you became more familiar with the subject.

(Richard)

Don't stop writing. We all reach a stage where our minds just go blank so just take a step away from your writing but return to it later the same day or very soon after. It is helpful to read over it again and again so that ideas will start to flow. If all else fails ask a friend to come and sit with you, explain what it is you are doing and ask them to read what you have done so far.

(Mary)

Do not be afraid to ask questions, I know it sounds a little pathetic, and many of the students in my class hate it when I do, but if I have a relevant question I will ask it, because there may be someone else in the class who may be thinking the same thing but is too shy to ask. You are there because you want to achieve, so do not be afraid to ask. It is how we learn.

(Mike)

From personal and observed experiences, back up your work as many times as you can, whether on memory stick, portable hardrives, disks, e-mailing it to yourself, back it up! You never know when the blue screen of death will appear. Cover yourself and ensure you have spares and at the same time ensure your spares are up to date also. Ensure you save clearly, in the sense of understandable document names and folders. This makes it easier to find them when the time comes to print.

(James)

Save as you go. I developed a level of paranoia about losing my work so I tended to save my work on to my laptop and once again on to a memory stick. In this way if something goes wrong with either method of saving work, I had a backup copy. I got into the habit of saving my work every half an hour to both copies. As a word of caution, students need to be aware that poor data management will not be accepted as an excuse for errors in submitted work or failure to submit work.

(Mary)

There are always people at the university who can help you.

(Dasha)

If you have been lucky enough to have a tutor that will read through any drafts make the best use of this opportunity. You will have been given marking criteria for written work. Use this information to gauge where to focus your efforts and measure your work against the set criteria.

(Mary)

Students will be penalised for late submission of any work. To reiterate, it is worth giving yourself plenty of time to make sure you get the written assignment completed in good time and in immaculate condition.

(Mary)

For prospective students who have been away from education for some time I recommend refreshing your English and numeracy skills either online or at a participating library or attend one of their support centres for face-to-face advice.

(Mike)

Hints and tips

- The importance of planning when writing cannot be underestimated.
- You should save your work regularly to avoid all your work being lost.
- Think about your motivations to succeed in your writing.
- Make use of advice and tips on how to organise your work effectively.
- Make the most of the support and help available in universities.

9

Eight simple rules for writing in health and social care

Hazel M, Chapman, June Keeling and Julie Williams

Introduction

Writing is a creative process. It transforms your own view of the world and enables you to grow and develop. This is why it is so commonly used as an assessment method, as educationalists use it to help you develop a more sophisticated understanding of your field in health and social care.

In this book we have attempted to provide you with simple tools to improve your writing skills and achieve your professional goals. We have aimed to inspire you with insights into how you can use writing to help you think more deeply and flexibly about the world and how that knowledge can improve you as a practitioner. While writing and learning are refined over many years, there are some ideas in this book that can change your thoughts, feelings and behaviours quite simply and quickly, and open your mind to the simple pleasure of writing.

In this concluding chapter we highlight a few of these hints and tips, and guide you to the relevant chapters to read more about them. We have identified eight simple rules for writing in health and social care.

Table 9.1 How to start writing

1 Be creative: write letters, stories, observations, your dreams and aspirations. This will free your mind and make it easier to apply yourself to professional and academic writing.
2 Limit the time you have to write: it is less daunting, and you will feel a sense of achievement.
3 Keep a notebook with you at all times to jot down your ideas.
4 Buy yourself (or suggest gifts of) attractive pens, pencils and notebooks.
5 Use pictures, diagrams, mind maps or audio-recordings of your ideas to get you started.
6 Write your name at the top of the page and then one sentence: it doesn't matter if you need to rewrite it later.
7 Think of yourself as a writer. Tell people you are writing, and emphasise the importance of writing in achieving your life goals.
8 Make writing enjoyable: choose or make your environment pleasant and reward yourself for every achievement.
9 If you prefer to write using a computer, invest in something portable and easy to use.
10 Write everywhere and anywhere, and write every day.

Rule 1 Write

This is the only way to become a better writer. Writing is a skill that can be learned and improved through practice and feedback on performance. As with any skill, it takes time and effort to develop, but your effort will give you confidence in your writing ability. Confident writing will make it easier for you to learn the theory and practice of professional health and social care. As you have seen throughout the book, writing is important for many reasons, but the more you write in any setting, the better your writing will become. Table 9.1 lists some ideas to get you started (see Chapter 2 for more).

Rule 2 Plan your writing

By just sitting down and writing, you have freed yourself from inhibition, allowing you to express all your ideas and make connections between them. This is a very good start, but now you need to structure it, make sure it answers the assessment brief or report requirements and organise it into ideas (paragraphs) that flow from one to the next in order to form a conclusion.

> ### Activity 9.1 The ten-minute plan
>
> Have a look at your next writing assignment. Spend five minutes writing down all your ideas, then organise them in an order that makes sense. Does it answer the brief? Are there gaps in your knowledge? Do you need to relate it more to practice? Make a note of the things you need to find out in order to finish your plan and put more detail in it.

Rule 3   Proofread and edit your writing

Every stage of the writing process is important. Proofreading to spot errors in spelling, punctuation, grammar and sentence structure is essential. However, on its own it is not enough. Once you have written your essay, reflection, report or other written work, you then need to edit it. This means reading carefully and rewriting to achieve the following:

- Eradicate unnecessary words.
- Shorten sentences.
- Organise sentences and paragraphs so that the points you make form a logical argument.
- Signpost the points you make so that the reader can follow your argument.

Sometimes, if you are having difficulty getting started, editing the work you have done can help you to remember your thoughts and stimulate new ideas about your writing. It is always a good idea to finish your assignments well in advance, as this final stage in the writing process is vital if you are going to achieve your potential and improve your performance

> ### Activity 9.2 Well begun is only half done
>
> Take a piece of writing that you have started (or an old piece of writing). If you are using a hard copy, use a different coloured

pencil or pen to edit. If you are using an electronic copy, use the Track Changes or similar facility on your computer. Read it all the way through, making note of any awkward phrases, waffle, errors in writing style or lack of clarity. Cross out anything you want to remove and put an asterisk or comment by anything you want to change. Go through your writing line by line correcting and improving it. You will find Chapter 3 a useful guide for this process. Now compare the two pieces of writing and see how much better your work is once edited. You will never submit your work unedited once you have tried this.

Rule 4   Look it up

If you have read Chapter 4, you will know that the level and quality of your writing can be improved by using evidence to support your explanations, arguments and conclusions. Quite soon, you will be aiming to analyse the validity of conclusions in the literature, evaluate their relative merits for application to the service user or situation you are writing about and even synthesise new perspectives by deriving knowledge from one arena and applying it in a different setting. None of this can be done without relevant reading and writing notes for your assignment.

Activity 9.3 What should your writing do?

In the table below, look up each type of writing in Chapter 4 and identify what you need to do in order to achieve that level of writing in your assignments

Writing style	What it entails
Description	
Explanation	
Argument	
Analysis	
Evaluation	
Synthesis	

Write little notes to yourself about how you can write at each level, and make sure your writing is at the level required for assessment. Never forget to read relevant textbooks to gain an understanding of the topic before you try to develop your knowledge to a higher level.

Rule 5   Reflect

To write well you need to reflect and make sure you plan how you will use your learning to improve your practice, as well as using trigger questions raised in practice to explore the relevant knowledge base. See Chapter 5 for guidance on why and how to reflect to develop your learning in theory and practice.

Activity 9.4 Reflection on writing performance and feedback

Think about the last piece of writing that you received feedback on.

1 What happened when you were writing it (what did you do/what didn't you do)?

2 What did the feedback say?

3 What do you think it means? Look up any words or ideas in your feedback that you are not sure of.

4 What will you do next time to improve your writing?

Rule 6   Record the care you give

It is important that you keep records about the care that you give when in practice. Documentation should be timely, accurate and concise in order to provide information for other professionals to use and ensure continuity of care. It should be discussed with the service user wherever possible, in order to promote personal control over health and social well-being.

Tips for improving your record keeping

- Read your qualified colleagues' care records to see how they write them.
- Offer to write up records under mentor supervision.
- Read your professional guidelines and local policies on record-keeping requirements.
- Stick to facts and use objective terminology (e.g. describe someone's behaviour rather than saying 'he was anxious').
- Imagine you were taking over the care for this person and wanted to know what had happened so far.
- If you are unable to access the records throughout the care period, keep confidential notes for recording later (then destroy the temporary notes).
- Remember that documentation could be used for audits and for legal purposes, so maintain professional standards of language and views expressed.
- Clear and accurate communication is the basis of good care, so keep practising.

See Chapter 6 for more ideas on good record keeping.

Rule 7   Prepare

Whatever format you present your work in, you need to prepare it. Consider your audience. How can you communicate your ideas in a fresh and interesting way? Here are some suggestions.

Communicating ideas

- Use pictures, diagrams and charts to illustrate your ideas.
- Keep the layout clear and uncluttered.
- Design posters and presentations to be colourful and striking, but also clear and unfussy.
- When presenting to others, remember to relate to them as human beings, using eye contact, facial expressions and movement to communicate your ideas.

- Think about audience participation – get them involved by asking questions or initiating short, simple activities related to your subject.
- Practise presentations, time yourself, and ask for feedback on written and presented work.
- Imagine the questions that might be asked and make notes on possible answers.
- Talk to the clock. Keep practising until you are sure the clock can understand all the important ideas in the time limit.

See Chapter 7 for lots of helpful hints and tips on a wide variety of ways to present your work. Whatever you do, commit yourself to doing it well – the more effort you put into assignments of any kind, the more knowledge, experience and confidence you will gain. See Chapter 8 for advice from students who have been through their health and social care programmes and have overcome their own challenges to gain their professional and academic qualifications.

Rule 8   Enjoy yourself

Writing should be fun. Take your mind out for an airing and be creative. Even though writing has a serious purpose, if you take it too seriously you will inhibit your creativity.

Activity 9.5 Fun ways to write

Choose one of the following ideas and use it to get started on something you need to write.

- Imagine you are writing it as a story for a six-year-old child – make it as simple, funny (or scary) as you can.
- Use coloured pens, cut-out pictures and produce a storyboard relating the ideas you want to write about.
- Take your notebook and pens and sit somewhere interesting – on summer days, by a river or in a park; on cold days, in a museum or café.

- Set a timer for a short time period (five or ten minutes) and write down all your ideas or set yourself the goal of writing a whole paragraph.
- Imagine you are a senior lecturer or practitioner teaching a student and write things in a way that you would understand them.
- Turn your ideas into a recipe – list all the key points as ingredients, identify all the processes involved in producing the desired professional and/or theoretical outcome.

Once you've finished this chapter, why not have a go at the crossword at the end – the previous chapters will help you to complete it.

Final thoughts

Everyone who has written in this book has had to learn how to write for health and social care. We all want you to benefit from our experience so that you can learn to write a little more easily and with fewer setbacks than you would otherwise. We hope you will continue to dip into this book whenever you need inspiration or fresh ideas to stimulate the writing process and we wish you all good things for your professional and academic future. Your contribution to the lives of others is important, and we hope that this book will help you to achieve the qualifications you need to become the best possible practitioner.

Our aim in this book has been to help you develop your writing skills and assist you in achieving your professional and academic goals. Important as these goals are though, they are not the only reason for writing. Writing is a creative process that allows you to rehearse being the person you want to become and develop your views of the world, in a process of growth that will continue long after you gain your qualification. Writing allows you to express your ideas and communicate with your professional community on an equal footing. While the ideas in this book can help you to write with greater skill, confidence and accuracy, it is only by writing on a regular basis, and responding to feedback on your writing, that you will achieve your potential. You are the only person who can make it happen, so start writing now.

Writing in health and social care – a crossword

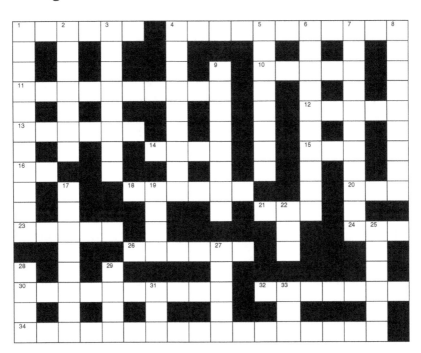

Across

1 Something you have earned when you write – it should be built into your writing (6).

4 Using a phrase or sentence to prepare the reader for the direction of your argument (11).

10 An example of a preposition or joining word. It means the opposite of below (5).

11 We can learn by reflecting on this (10).

12 The heading put at the beginning of a piece of writing (5).

13 Just because a word is . . ., that does not make it better (6).

14 Glasper's No ELBOW . . . (4).

15 Links in a reflection mind map may take you . . . to other thoughts (3).

16 In e-mail subject line, used to identify the previous e-mail it refers to. Literally 'the thing' in Latin (2).

18 People who speak this language may learn their way around Paris more easily (6).

20 Printers and pens use this (3).
21 Help! Another acronym (3).
23 Set achievable ones to reduce your task down to size (5).
24 Colloquial (and unprofessional) word for mouth (3).
26 Basic writing . . . you need them to write in health and social care (6).
30 A complex intellectual skill that involves judging the value or merit of something, using a questioning approach (10).
32 Verb in the third person past tense – anticipated or expected, as in: 'He . . . his assessment results cautiously' (7).
34 Applies to the processing of personal information, including the person's rights to confidentiality, accuracy of records about them and access to records about them (4, 10, 3).

Down

1 Gaining knowledge – the first step on Bloom's revised taxonomy of learning (11).
2 Can be a useful source of information online – every professional organisation has one. Make sure you use credible ones, though (3, 4).
3 Recover knowledge from your memory (8).
4 You need to put this on legal documents that you write in (9).
5 An essential part of the writing process – without it, you may not succeed (8).
6 Text reduction to be avoided at all costs. These can cause confusion in documentation (5, 5).
7 Critical analysis of other people's reasons can involve . . . their reasons and conclusions (11).
8 A text that helps you to find your way around an unknown place or new subject (9).
9 This should be logical and easy to follow, particularly when using a poster format (8).
17 Mrs Edwina Smith, in Writing for Practice, could become one of these if she brings a civil case for negligence against the service provider. In this case, the nurse's record would become a legal document (8).
19 'An inability to build life skills as a result of learning from our experiences puts us at . . . ' (Jasper 2003) (4).
22 Who's work should it be to avoid plagiarism? Not others' but your . . . (3).
25 In a sentence, it has something done to it (6).

27 The form of reasoning that must be valid in order for the conclusions to be accepted. One branch of philosophy. Rationality (5).

28 You need to do this so you can learn more about relevant topics for your writing (4).

29 An acronym for a surgical procedure sometimes used to treat benign prostatic hyperplasia – not to be used in written records (4).

31 The correct way to write 2 (3).

33 . . ., what, when, where, why – the five questions of information gathering. Can be a useful start to writing a reflection (3).

¹R	E	²W	A	³R	D		⁴S	I	G	N	⁵P	O	⁶S	T	⁷I	N	⁸G
E		E		E			I				L		H		D		U
M		B		T		G		⁹S		¹⁰A	B	O	V	E			I
¹¹E	X	P	E	R	I	E	N	C	E		N		R		N		D
M		A		I		A		Q		N		¹²T	I	T	L	E	
¹³B	I	G	G	E	R		T		U		I		F		I		B
E		E		V		¹⁴R	U	L	E		N		¹⁵O	F	F		O
¹⁶R	E		E		R		N		G		R		Y			O	
I		¹⁷C		¹⁸F	¹⁹R	E	N	C	H		M		²⁰I	N	K	
N		L		I		E		²¹S	²²O	S		N			
²³G	O	A	L	S		S			W			²⁴G	²⁵O	B	
	I		²⁶S	K	I	L	²⁷L	S		N			B	
²⁸R	M	²⁹T			O						J	
³⁰E	V	A	L	U	A	³¹T	I	N	G		³²A	³³W	A	I	T	E	D
A	N	R	w		I			H			C	
³⁴D	A	T	A	P	R	O	T	E	C	T	I	O	N	A	C	T	

DOING A LITERATURE REVIEW IN HEALTH AND SOCIAL CARE
A Practical Guide
Second Edition

Helen Aveyard

9780335238859 (Paperback)
2010

eBook also available

This bestselling book is a step-by-step guide to doing a literature review in health and social care. It is vital reading for all those undertaking their undergraduate or postgraduate dissertation or any research module which involves a literature review.

The new edition has been fully updated and provides a practical guide to the different types of literature that you may be encountered when undertaking a literature review.

Key features:

- Includes examples of commonly occurring real life scenarios encountered by students
- Provides advice on how to follow a clearly defined search strategy
- Details a wide range of critical appraisal tools that can be utilised

www.**openup**.co.uk

OPEN UNIVERSITY PRESS
McGraw - Hill Education

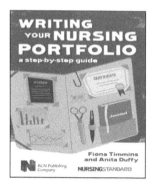

WRITING YOUR NURSING PORTFOLIO
A Step-by-step Guide

Fiona Timmins and Anita Duffy

9780335242849 (Paperback)
April 2011

eBook also available

This book is perfect for nurses who need to do a portfolio and don't know where to start. It explains simply what a portfolio can and cannot include, gives examples of good and bad pieces and demystifies the portfolio for the busy nurse. This is an essential purchase for qualified nurses doing PREP, and those studying who need a portfolio for assessment.

Key features:

- Provides suggested activities and tasks that can be completed and put into a portfolio
- Written as a 'step by step' guide
- Answers all the common questions nurses have about writing their portfolio

www.**openup**.co.uk

OPEN UNIVERSITY PRESS
McGraw - Hill Education

A BEGINNER'S GUIDE TO CRITICAL THINKING AND WRITING IN HEALTH AND SOCIAL CARE

Helen Aveyard, Pam Sharp and Mary Woolliams

9780335243662 (Paperback)
August 2011

eBook also available

Ever wondered what critical thinking is and how you can do it?

Ever struggled to write a critical essay?

Then this is the book for you. This is a beginner's guide to the skills of critical thinking, critical writing and critical appraisal in health and social care, and talks you through every stage of becoming a critical thinker. Each chapter tackles a different aspect of the process and using examples and simple language shows you how it's done. An essential purchase for students and qualified healthcare staff alike.

www.**openup**.co.uk

A BEGINNER'S GUIDE TO EVIDENCE BASED PRACTICE IN HEALTH AND SOCIAL CARE

Second Edition

Helen Aveyard and Pam Sharp

9780335246724 (Paperback)
April 2013

eBook also available

Have you heard of 'evidence based practice' but don't know what it means? Are you having trouble relating evidence to your practice?

This is the book for anyone who has ever wondered what evidence based practice is or how to relate it to practice. Fully updated in this brand new edition, this book is simple and easy to understand – and designed to help those new to the topic to apply the concept to their practice and learning with ease.

Key features:

- Additional material on literature reviews and searching for literature
- Even more examples for health and social care practice
- Extra material on qualitative research and evidence based practice
- Expanded section on hierarchies of evidence and how to use them

www.**openup**.co.uk

OPEN UNIVERSITY PRESS
McGraw - Hill Education